END TIMES

REVEALED

DAWN OF THE ANTICHRIST

DONNY BUDINSKY

EDITED BY: JESSICA BUDINSKY

STANDING FOR TRUTH MINISTRIES

END TIMES

REVEALED

DAWN OF THE ANTICHRIST

DONNY BUDINSKY

EDITED BY: JESSICA BUDINSKY

STANDING FOR TRUTH
MINISTRIES

Let no man deceive you by any means: for that day shall not come, except there come a falling away first, and that man of sin be revealed, the son of perdition;

Who opposeth and exalteth himself above all that is called God, or that is worshipped; so that he as God sitteth in the temple of God, shewing himself that he is God.

2 Thessalonians 2:3-4 [KJV]

All Scripture quotations, unless otherwise indicated, are taken from the King James Bible.

https://standingfortruthministries.com/

Other books by the Author

Special Creation - Dismantling Evolution and Confirming Independent Origins

The Endogenous Retrovirus Handbook - Dismantling the Best Evidence for Common Descent

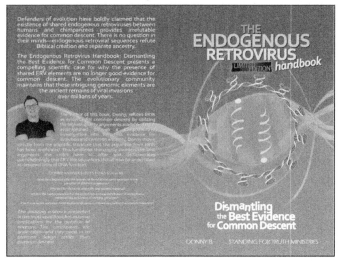

TABLE OF CONTENTS

INTRODUCTION

As Christians—we look forward to the return of our Lord and Savior Jesus Christ. This is our blessed hope. I have chosen to write this book to prepare Christians for this amazing day. There are several critical events that need to take place before the second coming of Jesus Christ. Unfortunately—there exist many erroneous positions that undermine Christian preparation. Believers need to be ready for the coming global power with its one world dictator. There will be a time of great tribulation prior to the coming of the Lord. An unholy trinity will be manifested in the last days.

The unholy, or false trinity, will wage war against God and the saints. They will establish a one world government, or a **New World Order**. There will be a one world religion—and a one world currency (instituted through the mark of the beast). The path has been set for the Antichrist to take power and become leader of the beast system. We are witnessing for the first time in human history, a collective movement that is global in character. This is one of the numerous reasons why every Christian needs this book. This book will provide a comprehensive model of Biblical eschatology (the study of last things) that will prepare my fellow brothers and sisters in Christ for the last days. The eschatological standpoint I will be representing in this book is "post-tribulation, pre-wrath". This perspective is Biblical (as I will demonstrate throughout this book), and will ensure believers are prepared for the age of the

1

Antichrist, the great tribulation, and the second coming of Jesus Christ.

CONSISTENT BIBLICAL HERMENEUTICS

The "post-tribulation, pre-wrath" view of end times is the result of sound Biblical hermeneutics (Bible interpretation). False eschatological positions are the result of sloppy hermeneutics and a bad approach to studying this significant topic. How do we properly study end times theology? Firstly—the New Testament should be paramount when studying eschatology. The book of Revelation (found in the New Testament) is key to understanding the last days. The New Testament is clear and mostly understandable. I say "mostly" because there are some harder texts to interpret—but when we take what we know, and interpret the more difficult to understand texts in light of the easier to understand ones, we avoid confusion and inconsistencies. There have been many wrong interpretations of important passages related to end times—but the reader can be confident in knowing this book will provide incredibly detailed and sophisticated explanations for texts such as 2 Thessalonians 2:7, Daniel 9:27, and other controversial passages.

An essential approach to remaining consistent in interpreting Bible prophecy, and end times theology is to first focus on the book of Revelation, followed by the epistles, and then the Gospels. The New Testament is paramount, and we must not contradict the clear eschatological scriptures of the New Testament with cryptic passages in the Old Testament.

There are passages in Old Testament books (such as Daniel—which chapter 2 of this book covers in detail, Ezekiel, and Jeremiah) that contain many points of prophecy that don't actually have an analogue in the New Testament. This should tell us that these points may not have any real significance in end times events. I am not saying the entirety of these books contain no passages with future significance. I am simply saying some passages. It is important that we don't take prophetic passages that have already been fulfilled, and incorrectly apply them to end times events. The positions I will be thoroughly refuting in this book are guilty of this—among many other things I will touch on.

There are many prophecies that have dual and triple fulfillments—with an immediate application for that day—and a future one. But some prophecies in the Old Testament may have only contained one application (or a second application at the first coming of Jesus), and therefore no future significance. These are all important aspects we must consider when studying end times theology. These points, plus many more, have been taken into serious consideration in the writing of this book. I truly believe the reader will be astounded at how consistent the "pre-wrath" model is, and will finish this book with a far greater understanding of the last days. My prayer is that this book edifies the body of Christ, and helps my brothers and sisters grow in faith and love for God's amazing Word.

THE NEW WORLD ORDER

The end times beast system is a one world government, a one world religion, and a one world financial system. The rise of this final kingdom—a worldwide kingdom—is predicted in the Bible. We can see Bible prophecy being fulfilled around us. Even many nonbelievers acknowledge where this world is heading—towards a New Order. This planet is currently composed of separate nations. These sovereign nations are not all merged under one global power. The same thing is true with religions. There are numerous religions in the world: Christianity, Islam, Hinduism, and Buddhism—just to name a few. There are also many financial systems. All over the world, we have countries with different currencies. Therefore, when we speak of a New World Order—the type of global power the Bible speaks of—we are talking about a world comprising one government, one religion, and one major financial system.

The Bible tells us this global entity will consist of one major ruler—and this ruler is the Antichrist. This man will unite the world through promises of peace. The elites will claim that it is the world's responsibility to come together for a better future. The Bible—God's Word—informs us that the merging of these nations and continents will not bring in peace—rather, it is a way for the dragon (Satan) and his elitist minions to gain full control, and power over the world. The coming Antichrist and this one world power is the last stage in Satan's war against God. There have been a long series of events all throughout history that have set the stage for this final act. This is the dragon's endgame.

As Christians, we know who will win in the end. The man of sin—the Antichrist—will be defeated. He will be cast into the lake of fire along with the dragon, and the false prophet—who together make up the false trinity. Jesus Christ will establish His Kingdom on this earth where He will rule with a rod of iron. The saints will rule with Him. This cosmic battle between good and evil—between God and the devil—will culminate with Jesus Christ coming back to this earth (with His saints) to destroy the unholy trinity.

The Lamb of God came to this earth the first time during a time when the Roman empire ruled the known world (1st century AD). He will come back the second time during the last days when the Antichrist and his one world government rule the entire planet. *The stage is set already for the dawn of the Antichrist.*

This book will take the reader on a journey through the end times. Many important questions pertaining to the last days will be answered. I have structured this book in a way that provides readers with a comprehensible reading experience. Everything leading up to the final chapter—Age of the Antichrist—will greatly help in setting a path that allows readers to fully understand how the Antichrist is revealed—and how these last days will play out. The contents of this book will assist in preparing believers for the coming tribulation.

OVERVIEW

There are many different eschatological camps. It is a hotly debated topic. It will be helpful to spend some time going over the various positions in the world of end times theology. This will assist the reader in better understanding the contents of this book.

A good place to start is the Millennium. Regarding the Millennium—there are groups who are premillennial, post-millennial, and amillennial. The premillennial view believes that Jesus Christ will literally return to this earth to rule and reign for 1000 years. Believers will rule and reign with Christ. Chapter 20 (including other passages in the Bible) of the book of Revelation very clearly teaches this position. The post-millennial and amillennial views have completely different views than the pre-millennial position (the Biblical position), and actually overlap in quite a lot of ways. Where the premillennialists believe that Jesus Christ will literally return to this earth for 1000 years—the postmillennialists (Jesus will return after the Millennium) and amillennialists believe the 1000-year reign is more figurative than literal. Some would purport that Jesus Christ is figuratively and symbolically ruling and reigning right now.

The curious aspect of Revelation chapter 20 is that the devil is locked up in hell for 1000 years in order that he no longer deceives the nations. The devil is not currently bound in hell for 1000 years. Clearly—the nations are deceived today. People are deceived. People have been blinded by the devil and his minions—but we as God's elect can remove the blinders by preaching the Gospel. The devil walks around this earth and he does so like a roaring lion seeking those whom he may devour. The Bible makes this absolutely clear. There is no evidence that we are currently in a millennial reign—or that the millennial reign has passed.

Postmillennialists hold to a position that basically says we as Christians will bring in the Millennium, and we will do this by preaching the Gospel and winning the lost to Christ. Essentially—they believe the world will slowly turn Christian. They see the world as getting better—rather than getting worse—even though the world is clearly going downhill—and downhill rather quickly. Once the world is primarily Christian—Jesus Christ will return (according to post-millennialism). This is an incredibly bizarre position—especially given how un-Christian the world is becoming. We see the stage set for a one world government, a one world religion, and a one world currency. There is no evidence that there will be a worldwide conversion to Christianity before the return of Jesus Christ.

These 3 millennial views are a helpful way to break down the various views on eschatology. Within the premillennial view (the Biblically supported view), there exist those that believe the rapture will occur before the tribulation—and those that believe (correctly) that Jesus returns **after the tribulation**. This is where the more sophisticated debate takes place. Both the post-millennial and amillennial views are extremely difficult to take seriously. They are very unsophisticated—and incredibly unscriptural positions. As a matter of fact—they are downright indefensible. This will be demonstrated throughout the book.

Another false and easily debunked position is preterism (which takes many forms). Preterism is basically an idea that claims Biblical prophecy (including Revelation) has mostly been fulfilled. Preterists would argue for the events of 70 AD as largely being the fulfillment of Bible prophecy. These events would include the destruction of the Jewish temple at the hands of Titus and the Roman army, and the dispersion of the Jewish people into all parts of the world. Pre- and post-tribulation rapture proponents are considered futurists. A futurist places Bible prophecies involving the great tribulation, the return of Jesus Christ, and the Millennium as being future whereas preterists argue these events have already taken place (depending on the flavor of preterism).

There are different versions of preterism. These versions include both partial and full preterism. A partial preterist may say the second coming and the judgment of the dead are future, but that the great tribulation and the events associated with it have occurred in and around 70 AD. The full preterist ultimately claims everything has happened, including the second coming of Jesus Christ. Futurists are therefore neither preterist or historicist (another false position). A historicist would basically argue that most of the events in Revelation and Bible prophecy have happened throughout history with many of these events found in Biblical prophecy being figurative and symbolic—rather than literal. Historicists like to argue the days provided in scripture that are associated with Daniel's 70th week (1260, 1290, 42 months, etc.) represent years, and not literal days. This absurd claim will be debunked in subsequent chapters. Both major

8

preterist positions (partial and full) will be dismantled throughout this book. Whether it's a preterist position that says most Bible prophecies have been fulfilled (with only a few left to be accomplished) or a preterist view that claims all prophecies have been fulfilled, there are still serious errors that need to be addressed. And they will be addressed.

This is just a brief breakdown of the various eschatological positions. As I have stated, this book will defend the post-tribulation, pre-wrath rapture model of eschatology. It will focus heavily on refuting arguments against this Biblical position as well as extensively rebutting the pre-tribulation rapture position.

There are major dangers involved in the post-millennial and amillennial views—and even the pre-tribulation rapture view. This is because the Bible clearly teaches the Antichrist will show up on the scene prior to the return of Jesus Christ. This makes those holding to the above false positions or erroneous views of end times theology as being vulnerable to accepting the Antichrist and wrongfully believing he is the second coming of Jesus. Proponents of the pre-wrath view of end times know to expect the Antichrist before the second coming of Jesus Christ. The Antichrist will have a mass appeal—since the Bible states the whole world will worship after him. This means he will be convincing. We must be awake and watchful. The post-tribulation, pre-wrath view prepares believers for the arrival of the Antichrist. We know that the imposter arrives prior to Jesus Christ. As a matter of fact—Paul warns believers that if anybody tells you the rapture can occur before the revealing of the Antichrist, they are deceiving you. Do not believe them.

LET NO MAN DECEIVE YOU

The verses in 2 Thessalonians 2:1-4 remove any possibility of a pre-tribulation rapture. As a matter of fact—pre-tribulation rapturists have an extremely difficult time explaining this verse from their end times model:

2 Thessalonians 2:1-4

2 Now we beseech you, brethren, **by the coming of our Lord Jesus Christ**, and by our **gathering together unto him**,

[2] That ye be not soon shaken in mind, or be troubled, neither by spirit, nor by word, nor by letter as from us, as that **the day of Christ** is at hand.

[3] Let no man deceive you by any means: **for that day shall not come**, except there come a falling away first, and that man of sin be revealed, the son of perdition;

[4] Who opposeth and exalteth himself above all that is called God, or that is worshipped; so that he as God sitteth in the temple of God, shewing himself that he is God.

(Emphasis mine)

Note: Many scriptures will be used throughout this book. **Emphasis** in each scriptural citation will be mine. This is to help the reader better understand the specific point I am making.

I engaged in a formal debate (*The Great Rapture Debate | Pre-Trib vs. Post-Trib/Pre-Wrath*) with a pre-tribulation rapturist named JD Morin. He challenged me to a debate at the beginning of **August 2022**, and we officially had the debate on **September 26th 2022.** Having engaged in nearly 100 (as of September 2022) formal debates (mainly on the creation versus evolution topic), I obviously could not turn down this opportunity to demonstrate the strength of the post-tribulation, pre-wrath rapture in a live debate against somebody defending the pre-tribulation rapture doctrine (I should add, it is very difficult finding pre-tribulation rapturists willing to engage in formal debate). This debate can be viewed online.

What sparked this debate is an ongoing End Times Theology series I have been working diligently on and releasing (several episodes a month), that includes an open-mic panel discussion/debate where Dr. Kent Hovind and I (both of whom hold to a rapture position that is after the tribulation, but with differing views on aspects within the post-tribulation, pre-wrath position) engaged several individuals of opposing views (these views include partial preterism and pre-tribulation rapture). This specific panel discussion has accumulated thousands of views (with the End Times Theology series also accumulating thousands of views), and has resulted in a lot of feedback and interest in this important topic. Both the open-mic discussion and the series itself can be viewed online (this includes the Standing For Truth Ministries official website).

Website - https://standingfortruthministries.com/

Now why am I mentioning all this? This is because a significant part of the discussion portion of my formal debate with JD Morin focused on this passage (2 Thessalonians 2:1-4). My interlocutor admitted this was a difficult passage for him to explain. The reason this passage is essentially impossible for the defenders of a pre-tribulation rapture to explain is because it is plainly refuting the claim that the coming of the Lord (the rapture event) can occur at any moment—or before several events take place.

The teachings in 2 Thessalonians 2 are incredibly important to understand because Paul is teaching that the day of Christ cannot come until a few important events take place. This clearly indicates the rapture cannot come at any time—like many pre-tribulation rapturists will frequently say. They would teach you could be sitting in church one Sunday and could even be caught up that day (without any sign or any warning). But this is simply not true—since there are events that need to take place before the day of Christ. Paul is very adamant in this passage. He is warning believers not to be deceived. This is why this topic is incredibly important. Those that teach a pre-tribulation rapture are deceiving (many don't know that they are teaching a deceitful doctrine) believers into thinking they will escape the tribulation—and the arrival of the Antichrist.

Paul is saying even if you get a letter that appears to be from "us" saying that Jesus can come back at any moment—do not believe it. The saints are being told not to be deceived by any means. This is a serious warning. Verses 3 and 4 make it clear that the coming of the Lord (the rapture) cannot come until a falling away, and the revealing of the Antichrist (man of sin):

> ³ Let no man deceive you by any means: **for that day shall not come**, except there come a **falling away first**, and **that man of sin be revealed, the son of perdition**;
>
> ⁴ **Who opposeth and exalteth himself above all that is called God, or that is worshipped; so that he as God sitteth in the temple of God, shewing himself that he is God.**

These verses should be easy to understand. They are not cryptic or complicated. They are not confusing in any way. Paul is saying there are a few things that need to occur before the second coming of Jesus Christ. Firstly—there must be a falling away (a great apostasy). Secondly—the man of sin needs to be revealed. The man of sin is the Antichrist. The abomination of desolation is alluded to in verse 4:

⁴ Who opposeth and exalteth himself above all
that is called God, or that is worshipped; so that
he as God sitteth in the temple of God, shewing
himself that he is God.

Anybody who knows their Bible—and understands
basic eschatology—understands that the abomination of
desolation does not occur until roughly 3.5 years into the 70th
week of Daniel (this week totals 7 years). But pre-tribulation
rapturists would have us believe the rapture will take place
before the 70th week of Daniel! No—Paul is clearly teaching
the abomination of desolation must take place before the
second coming of Christ. This means the rapture cannot take
place until sometime after the 3.5-year mark of this 7 year
period! Are you beginning to see why these verses act to
decimate a pre-tribulation rapture?

The Antichrist will be revealed by standing in the
temple (a rebuilt 3rd temple in the last days) while claiming to
be God. He will also stop the newly instituted daily sacrifice.
Proponents of a pre-tribulation rapture cannot claim that Jesus
could come back at any moment—without any signs—on a
scriptural basis. The scriptures refute this claim. Jesus will not
come back at any moment because the abomination of
desolation (and a great falling away) needs to occur first.

The pre-tribulation rapture is a deception. It will leave
believers unprepared for the tribulation and the arrival of the
Antichrist. Those that are expecting the second coming of
Jesus prior to the Antichrist (since they believe the rapture
occurs prior to the end times 7-year period) are leaving
themselves open to being caught off guard when the Antichrist

comes first. We are told to be watchful. We are given signs to look out for. And the pre-tribulation rapture deception will leave Christians unprepared. This is one of the many reasons why this topic is so unbelievably important. And this is why I have chosen to write an entire book on it. If somebody tells you (even a brother or a sister in Christ) that the day of Christ is at hand (before a great falling away, and before the arrival of the Antichrist), don't believe them. They may not be willingly deceiving you (since many have unfortunately blindly believed in the pre-tribulation rapture without ever really looking into it), but it is important nonetheless to know this claim (that Jesus can come back prior to the tribulation) is false. I want my fellow brothers and sisters to be ready for the tribulation and the dawn of the Antichrist.

CHAPTER ONE

TO BE REVEALED

Revelation 1:1-3

1 The Revelation of Jesus Christ, which God gave unto him, to shew unto his servants things which must shortly come to pass; and he sent and signified it by his angel unto his servant John:

² Who bare record of the word of God, and of the testimony of Jesus Christ, and of all things that he saw.

³ Blessed is he that readeth, and they that hear the words of this prophecy, and keep those things which are written therein: for the time is at hand.

We see clearly what the purpose of the book of Revelation is. It is to "shew unto his servants things which must shortly come to pass." Revelation is primarily being written to the saved—those that have been passed from death unto life:

John 5:24

²⁴ Verily, verily, I say unto you, **He that heareth my word**, and **believeth on him that**

sent me, hath everlasting life, and shall not come into condemnation; but is passed from death unto life.

These things are written for God's elect to know what must shortly come to pass.

The book of Revelation literally means "to be revealed". We have this important book to reveal things to us. That which is laid out in Revelation is not to be obscure—or confusing—but to be understood. The book of Revelation is written that we should be ready for what's to come.

Unfortunately—many Christians have intentionally avoided the book of Revelation in their study. They have been taught that Revelation is difficult to understand, and is wrapped up in mystery. This is simply not true. Again—the book of Revelation is given to us that future events might be revealed. Those things written in Revelation that at first may appear to be a mystery—are quickly revealed to us as to what it means.

Revelation 1:20

[20]**The mystery of the seven stars** which thou sawest in my right hand, and the seven golden candlesticks. **The seven stars are the angels of the seven churches: and the seven candlesticks which thou sawest are the seven churches.**

Notice the mystery of the seven stars are immediately revealed to us. This is no longer a mystery. The book of Revelation does not have to be a mystery to us. It is meant to reveal things to us.

Sadly, numerous Christians go into interpreting the book of Revelation with preconceived ideas. They have been taught erroneously. There are many false eschatological (study of end times) positions that are contradictory to what Revelation teaches. Many of these positions (especially the pre-tribulation rapture doctrine) will be comprehensively refuted throughout this important book on the last days. If the reader will read this book objectively and with an open mind—they will undoubtedly know that the post-tribulation, pre-wrath eschatological model is the strongest.

Many teach that God's people (the elect) will not be here for the majority of events in Revelation. They erroneously teach that believers will be raptured out prior to the tribulation period. This would indicate that Revelation was written as a warning to unsaved people. This is false. Revelation is written for God's people to understand future events. These events include the tribulation period, the rapture, God's wrath, the Millennium, and the new heavens and new earth. This book will prove that believers are here on this earth for the tribulation. Believers will be here for the revealing of the Antichrist. God's elect will be raptured after the tribulation and before God's wrath. I will leave no stone unturned while demonstrating this directly from scripture. The Bible is the Word of God—and we need to believe what God's Word says in all things.

HE COMETH WITH CLOUDS

Those that hold to a pre-tribulation rapture unfortunately do not understand Revelation 1:7. A great way to understand end times events is to first understand that Jesus comes back with clouds. A failure to understand Revelation 1:7 will result in a failure to understand the entire book itself. This is where a lot of people go wrong in their interpretation of Revelation. We need to go into the final book of the Bible with the right view and understanding of Revelation 1:7 and the nature of Christ's second coming.

Revelation 1:7

⁷ Behold, **he cometh with clouds**; and **every eye shall see him**, and they also which pierced him: and all kindreds of the earth shall wail because of him. Even so, Amen.

As we can see in the above passage—Jesus Christ is coming back with clouds—and every eye shall see Him. This is not a secret rapture. No—this is an event that everybody will know about. There is nothing secret about the second coming of Christ.

Acts chapter 1 is known as the Ascension of Jesus Christ:

Acts 1:9-11

⁹ And when he had spoken these things, while they beheld, he was taken up; and **a cloud received him out of their sight**.

10 And while they looked stedfastly toward heaven as he went up, behold, two men stood by them in white apparel;

11 Which also said, Ye men of Galilee, **why stand ye gazing up into heaven? this same Jesus, which is taken up from you into heaven, shall so come in like manner as ye have seen him go into heaven.**

The first coming of Jesus Christ was in Bethlehem's manger. This was the birth of our Lord. This event took place roughly 2000 years ago. It was during this first coming that Jesus had His ministry, performed miracles, died on the cross, and rose from the dead in order that the world could be saved. Jesus conquered death and hell. In Acts chapter 1, Jesus is about to ascend into heaven where He will be seated at the right hand of the Father. The apostles watched as Jesus ascended and a cloud took Him out of their sight. This was an important historical moment that the apostles directly witnessed. Verse 11 makes it clear that Jesus will return in a similar manner that He left in. Jesus will come again—and He will come with clouds. Now I want the reader to shift their focus to an important passage in Matthew 24:

Matthew 24:29-31

29 **Immediately after the tribulation** of those days **shall the sun be darkened,** and **the moon shall not give her light,** and **the stars shall fall from heaven**, and **the powers of the heavens shall be shaken**:

³⁰And then shall appear the sign of the Son of man in heaven: and then shall all the tribes of the earth mourn, and **they shall see the Son of man coming in the clouds of heaven with power and great glory.**

³¹ **And he shall send his angels with a great sound of a trumpet**, and **they shall gather together his elect** from the four winds, from one end of heaven to the other.

In Matthew 24—we see a clear chronology of events. First, we see the **tribulation**, and then the **sun and moon are darkened** (signs in the heavens). Next, we see the **Son of man coming in the clouds of heaven.** This is **Jesus Christ**. This is the second coming of Jesus Christ. Jesus is coming in the clouds. This correlates perfectly with **Acts 1:9-11** and **Revelation 1:7**. This is a significant characteristic of the return of Jesus Christ. Jesus left in clouds—and He will come back in clouds.

After the tribulation—and after the sun and moon are darkened, Jesus Christ will come in the clouds to gather together His elect (believers). The word elect refers primarily to believers in the New Testament. To make this even stronger, let us incorporate the famous rapture passage into the equation:

1 Thessalonians 4:16-18

¹⁶ For the **Lord himself shall descend from heaven with a shout**, with the voice of the

archangel, and with **the trump of God**: and the dead in Christ shall rise first:

[17] Then we which are alive and remain shall be **caught up together with them in the clouds, to meet the Lord in the air**: and so shall we ever be with the Lord.

[18] Wherefore comfort one another with these words.

Notice how Paul in 1 Thessalonians 4:17 is informing the reader that the Lord will come in the clouds to catch up believers to be with Him. This beautifully connects with the other verses we have mentioned that describe Jesus leaving and coming in the clouds. I want the reader to see these important passages again. I will put them one after another for examination (*please see the end of the book for detailed charts*):

Acts 1:9-11

[9] And when he had spoken these things, while they beheld, he was taken up; and **a cloud received him out of their sight**.

[10] **And while they looked stedfastly toward heaven as he went up**, behold, two men stood by them in white apparel;

¹¹ Which also said, Ye men of Galilee, **why stand ye gazing up into heaven? <u>this same Jesus, which is taken up from you into heaven, shall so come in like manner as ye have seen him go into heaven.</u>**

Matthew 24:29-31

²⁹ Immediately after the tribulation of those days shall the sun be darkened, and the moon shall not give her light, and the stars shall fall from heaven, and the powers of the heavens shall be shaken:

<u>**³⁰And then shall appear the sign of the Son of man in heaven**</u>: and then shall all the tribes of the earth mourn, and **they shall see the Son of man coming in the clouds of heaven with power and great glory.**

³¹ And he shall send his angels with a great sound of a trumpet, and they shall gather together his elect from the four winds, from one end of heaven to the other.

Revelation 1:7

⁷ Behold, **he cometh with clouds**; and **every eye shall see him**, and they also which pierced him: and all kindreds of the earth shall wail because of him. Even so, Amen.

1 Thessalonians 4:16-18

[16] For the **Lord himself shall descend from heaven with a shout**, with the voice of the archangel, and with **the trump of God**: and the dead in Christ shall rise first:

[17] Then we which are alive and remain shall be **caught up together with them in the clouds, to meet the Lord in the air**: and so shall we ever be with the Lord.

[18] Wherefore comfort one another with these words.

By now, the reader should see the connection. Jesus left in clouds, and He will return in clouds. The rapture (being caught up together with Jesus Christ in the clouds) is after the tribulation—and before God's wrath. This could not be any clearer. Those that believe in a rapture that occurs before the tribulation will attempt desperately to disconnect the event in Matthew 24 from 1 Thessalonians 4 (the famous rapture passage). They will admit that Revelation 1:7, Acts 1:9, and 1 Thessalonians 4 are the rapture—but will then refuse to admit that Matthew 24:29-31 is the rapture—even though this is Jesus coming in the clouds. Remember—Jesus left with clouds—and He will return with clouds.

In the famed rapture passage, we see Jesus Christ coming in the clouds. We have a trumpet in 1 Thessalonians 4:16-18—which we likewise see in Matthew 24. What are the differences between the rapture passage in 1 Thessalonians and the gathering together of the elect in Matthew 24? The answer is basically there are no significant differences to where we can justify saying these are not the same events (the rapture). Those that reject a pre-wrath view of the rapture (and hold to the pre-tribulation view) have no real justification for saying 1 Thessalonians 4:16-18 is the rapture, but Matthew 24:29-31 isn't.

Defenders of the false pre-tribulation rapture only argue that Matthew 24:29-31 is not the rapture because of preconceived ideas. Anybody going into the Bible without a preconceived idea that the pre-tribulation rapture must be true will easily see that these events are the same. All of the important characteristics associated with the second coming of Jesus Christ are found in Matthew 24. Again—Jesus is coming in the clouds, the elect are gathered together in the air, and a trumpet is sounded.

The timing of the day of the Lord is the same as the timing of the rapture. They both are described as coming as a thief in the night (a thief to the unbelieving world). The day of the Lord is always associated with the sun and moon being darkened. We see the sun and moon darkened in Matthew 24:29:

> [29] Immediately after the tribulation of those days **shall the sun be darkened, and the moon shall not give her light**, and the stars shall fall from heaven, and the powers of the heavens shall be shaken:

In 1 Thessalonians 5:1-4, we see the day of the Lord mentioned in association with the second coming of Jesus Christ:

> **5** But of the times and the seasons, brethren, ye have no need that I write unto you.
>
> [2] For yourselves know perfectly that **the day of the Lord so cometh as a thief in the night.**
>
> [3] For when they shall say, Peace and safety; then sudden destruction cometh upon them, as travail upon a woman with child; and they shall not escape.
>
> **[4] But ye, brethren, are not in darkness, that that day should overtake you as a thief.**

1 Thessalonians 5:1-4

This indicates that all the critical elements or components associated with the second coming are present in Matthew 24—including the sun and moon being darkened (since the day of the Lord is linked with the sun and moon being darkened—which is mentioned in 1 Thessalonians 5:1-4).

In Paul's second letter to the Thessalonians, he attaches the second coming to our (believers) gathering unto him:

2 Thessalonians 2:1

2 Now we beseech you, brethren, by **the coming of our Lord Jesus Christ**, and by **our gathering together unto him**,

THAT DAY AND HOUR

In verse 36 of Matthew 24, "that day" is a reference to the day of the Lord—the rapture (when the sun and moon are darkened):

Matthew 24:32-36

[32] Now learn a parable of the fig tree; When his branch is yet tender, and putteth forth leaves, ye know that summer is nigh:

[33] So likewise ye, when ye shall see all these things, know that it is near, even at the doors.

[34] Verily I say unto you, This generation shall not pass, till all these things be fulfilled.

³⁵ Heaven and earth shall pass away, but my
words shall not pass away.

³⁶ But of **that day and hour** knoweth no man,
no, not the angels of heaven, but my Father
only.

Firstly—I want to quickly refute the preterist twisting
of verse 34. "This generation shall not pass" is a reference to
the generation that will begin to see these things take
place—meaning it will not be a prolonged period of time that
these events take place (100s of years). It will be in a single
generation that all these end times events take place and
culminate with the rapture. The preterist will attempt (and fail)
to say that the generation being referred to is the generation at
the time this was spoken (to the disciples). This is why they
place the great tribulation in 70 AD with the destruction of the
temple. This is clearly false—as I have just demonstrated. Did
Jesus Christ come in the clouds in 70 AD? Did the sun and
moon go dark? Did the trumpet and vial judgments (hail and
fire cast upon the earth, mountain cast into the sea, rivers
turned into blood, locusts wreaking havoc on the earth, etc.)
occur? Of course not.

Next, I want to refute an argument employed by
apologists of the pre-tribulation rapture. They argue that verse
36 is implying a pre-tribulation rapture. They claim this
because to them "that day and hour knoweth no man" means
Jesus could come back at any time—even before the
tribulation (even though Matthew 24:29 clearly says the
rapture is **AFTER** the tribulation). I find it rather amusing
they would apply such an argument pertaining to the rapture

29

when in fact these same pre-tribulation proponents will deny Matthew 24 is even talking about the rapture! If I said to you "that day", you would reasonably respond with "what day?" "That day" must be referring back to a day just talked about. And "that day" is referring to the day the sun and moon are darkened—the Day of the Lord—which is the second coming of Jesus Christ! This is how unsophisticated the level of argumentation is from the pre-tribulation rapture camp. They can't have it both ways. They want to say Matthew 24 isn't talking about the rapture and yet utilize an argument from verse 36 to say the rapture can occur anytime—and by anytime meaning before the rapture! This is absurd.

The day we are talking about in verse 36 is the rapture—the gathering together of the elect (believers). Matthew 24:29 is clear—the gathering together takes place after the tribulation. This means "that day" comes after the tribulation, and not before. Promoters of the pre-tribulation rapture are not consistent. They do not have a sophisticated eschatological model. As a matter of fact—those that use this argument to assert imminence are actually taking this verse out of context (especially since they refuse to acknowledge the previous verses are the rapture). We may not know the exact day or hour of the rapture—but one thing is certain—we know it is after the tribulation! This is what the Bible clearly says. Jesus said His second coming is after the tribulation—and as believers we need to believe this!

If I were planning a trip to my friend's house in the United States, and I told him I was coming after Christmas—but did not give him an exact date—would it make any sense to say, "Donny could come at any time"? Of course not. My friend can know that I am coming to visit after the summer and yet not know the exact date. The arguments being advanced by those that hold to a pre-tribulation rapture are illogical and result in confusion. Unfortunately—many people are confused today. There are too many people in churches (oftentimes really good churches!) who are being taught the pre-tribulation rapture. And because of this, they read Revelation and are confused. When they finally understand the rapture comes after the tribulation and before God's wrath, it is a relief to know that they can finally understand Bible prophecy and end times theology. God wants us to know what's to come. He wants us to be prepared! We as believers are told to watch. Would it make any sense to tell believers to watch for something that we will not be here for? No, it would not. We are to watch for the events that will occur prior to the second coming (the arrival of the Antichrist, world war, famine, etc.). The pre-wrath model of eschatology is both sophisticated and consistent. It allows for the believer to be watchful and confident in what's to come. Pre-wrath proponents can read Revelation and make it fit. The book makes sense.

THE DAY OF THE LORD AND THE RAPTURE

1 Thessalonians 4 is a popular passage. And it is a passage that destroys pretribulationism. This is especially true when we keep reading into chapter 5 of 1 Thessalonians (which many people forget to do). When we read both chapters, we see even more incredible proof that the rapture comes after the tribulation:

1 Thessalonians 5:1-4

5 But of the times and the seasons, brethren, ye have no need that I write unto you.

² For yourselves know perfectly **that the day of the Lord so cometh as a thief in the night.**

³ For when they shall say, Peace and safety; then sudden destruction cometh upon them, as travail upon a woman with child; and they shall not escape.

⁴ **But ye, brethren, are not in darkness, that that day should overtake you as a thief.**

Paul just finished discussing the rapture in 1 Thessalonians 4 (the famous rapture passage). Chapter 5 begins with what is called a **conjunction** (the word "But"). This tells us Paul is continuing his thought from what was just being said prior to chapter 5. 1 Thessalonians 5 is not moving onto a completely different topic. Essentially—Paul just finished describing the rapture (believers being caught up with Jesus Christ in the clouds), and now he is telling believers *"But of the times and the seasons, brethren, ye have no need that I write unto you."* Paul is clearly referring to the times and the seasons of the rapture. We know this because of the conjunction—the word "But".

Verse 2 of Chapter 5 also begins with a conjunction. What we are reading in this chapter is all one thought—and it is a thought continued from the content of 1 Thessalonians 4. **This is proof that the timing of the day of the Lord is the**

same timing as the rapture. Pre-tribulation rapturists want to assert (without evidence—as usual) that the day of the Lord and the rapture won't happen on the same day. Well—chapters 4 and 5 of Thessalonians dismantle this assertion. Paul tells us *"That the day of the Lord so cometh as a thief in the night."* And this is after he just got done telling the brethren about the rapture. If the day of the Lord took place at a different time than the rapture (as pre-tribulationists argue), this would make no sense. The only explanation that makes sense is that the day of the Lord and the rapture occur at the same time—or at least on the same day. This must be true for Paul to use the day of the Lord and the rapture in the same thought.

Paul is ultimately saying the timing of what was just talked about (the rapture in chapter 4) is the same timing as the day of the Lord, and you know that will come as a thief in the night (to the unprepared and unbelieving world). The day of the Lord happens on the same day as the rapture—and there is no way for defenders of the pre-tribulation rapture to get out of this reality. What many don't understand though—is that the day of the Lord is a day of judgment and wrath upon the earth and upon those that are unsaved. This wrath begins to be poured out on the same day the rapture takes place. To believers—this day is the day of Christ (a day of redemption and blessing), but to unbelievers—this day comes both unexpectedly and with great judgment.

We know the day of the Lord comes after the sun and moon darkened—and it has just been established that the day of the Lord and the rapture occur on the same day—which proves the rapture comes after the sun and moon are darkened—and after the tribulation. Pre-tribulation rapturism can be refuted in so many ways—and this is just one.

THE PRE-WRATH RAPTURE (HELPFUL CHARTS)

Here is a chart to help the reader better understand the pre-wrath rapture timeline:

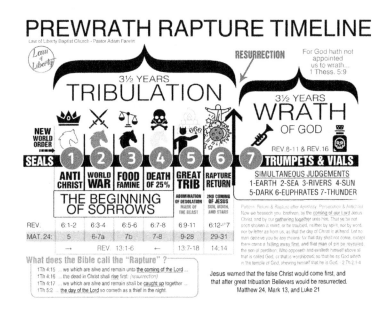

SOURCE: (2022). Lawoflibertybaptist.com. http://lawoflibertybaptist.com/prewrath.png

The next chart (created by Dr. Alan Kurschner) provides an additional visual to help the reader understand that Daniel's 70th week is not only composed of tribulation. The pre-wrath position understands we are dealing with a period of tribulation and a period of wrath, with the midpoint being the abomination of desolation (that starts the great tribulation):

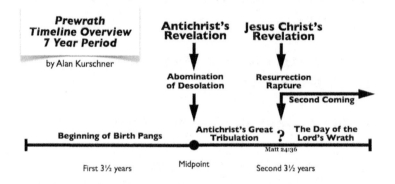

SOURCE: *What is Prewrath?* (2013, February 19).
ESCHATOS MINISTRIES.
https://www.alankurschner.com/2013/02/19/what-is-prewrath/

Note: I do not agree with all aspects of Dr. Alan Kurschner's eschatological model, but I do agree with enough of it to cite his charts and quote him when acceptable. I am very confident with the model I am presenting in this book. I may cite other pre-wrath proponents and scholars, but that does not necessarily mean I agree with everything they teach on eschatology (and of course other doctrines).

Although the previous 2 charts are very helpful, I strongly believe the next timeline chart is the best pre-wrath position (I can at this time find nothing I disagree with on it). Therefore, I recommend the reader frequently refer to this chart (and the previous charts) as they work through this comprehensive book. This will be highly beneficial in

understanding many of the technical points made throughout
this important book.

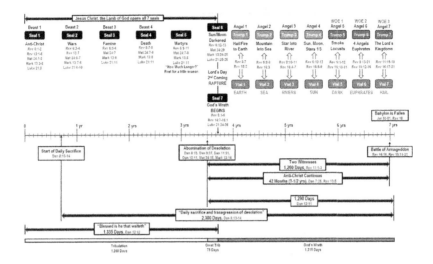

Note: For an enlarged look at this comprehensive and accurate
chart, please refer to the end of this book (**Visuals** section).

REVELATION 6

The only time in Revelation where the sun and moon are
darkened, and the stars fall from heaven, is in Revelation
6—at the sixth seal. This must be the event we read about in
Matthew 24, Luke 21, and Mark 13 (parallel passages). The
sun and moon are darkened at the opening of the sixth seal.
This is what the Bible refers to as the tribulation. Therefore,
everything that happens before the sixth seal is the tribulation,
and everything after the sixth seal is not the tribulation. The
tribulation period ends at the sixth seal (roughly 3.5 years into

Daniel's 70th week). The rapture has not and cannot occur until the sun and moon are darkened. We also know the rapture (coming of the Lord) cannot occur until the man of sin is revealed. Since the Antichrist will not officially be revealed until the abomination of desolation, the rapture cannot occur before the tribulation. The abomination of desolation occurs roughly 3.5 years into Daniel's 70th week (the 7 year end times period). This fact demolishes the pre-tribulation rapture, since pre-tribulation rapturists want the rapture to take place prior to the week even starting! It is impossible to fit a rapture event before the 7 years begins. The rapture must occur sometime after the abomination of desolation.

This all means that the rapture has not occurred in Revelation chapters 1 to 5. The rapture happens in Revelation 6 when the sun and moon are darkened—and those raptured (great multitude) appear in heaven in Revelation 7. This is exactly what we would expect to be the case if the pre-wrath position were true. We see tribulation in Revelation 6, sun and moon darkened at the sixth seal, and then the great multitude appearing in heaven in Revelation 7—with God's wrath being poured out after the tribulation, and after the rapture. This is all extremely consistent and fits incredibly well. Advocates of the pre-tribulation rapture cannot explain why this fits so well from the pre-wrath starting point. These are all realities consistent with what the pre-wrath rapture model would expect and predict.

The tribulation period does not go the entire 7 years of Daniel's 70th week (as some have erroneously argued). The tribulation ends at the sun and moon being darkened. The great tribulation starts at the abomination of desolation. The great tribulation is cut short for the elect's sake. This is because if the great tribulation were not cut short (the period of Daniel's 70th week where the Antichrist is revealed, the one world government is fully implemented, and the mark of the beast is made mandatory), no Christian would survive. For this reason, God cuts this time short, and Jesus Christ comes in the clouds at the rapture to save the elect (Matthew 24, Luke 21, Mark 13, Revelation 6 and 7).

God pours out His wrath after the tribulation—and after the rapture. This means Christians will not be on the earth during God's wrath. God pouring out His wrath is very different from the tribulation. Tribulation has to do with persecution. Tribulation is what man, and the devil, do to believers—and wrath is what God does to unbelievers. These are extremely different aspects to end times events.

Apologists of a pre-tribulation rapture confuse tribulation and wrath. They don't understand that tribulation and wrath are different. They will assert "believers are not appointed unto wrath". And they are right! Which is why believers are removed from this earth prior to God's wrath. This does not mean believers are removed prior to the tribulation—since again—tribulation and wrath are different aspects to this end times 7-year period (first half being tribulation and second half being God's wrath). This is why the most consistent eschatological position is the post-tribulation, pre-wrath rapture. The main events of Daniel's 70th week cover 7 years—but the entire 7 years is not tribulation. The tribulation covers roughly half of the 7-year period—with the remainder being God's wrath (culminating at the Millennium).

TRIBULATION AND WRATH—THERE IS A DIFFERENCE

Knowing the difference between tribulation and wrath is incredibly important when studying end times theology. Pre-tribulation rapture proponents wrongfully believe that tribulation and wrath are the same thing. This is why they will frequently argue for a pre-tribulation rapture by claiming God would never subject His children to wrath. They'll say God would not pour out His wrath on His own people (they assume the entire 7-year period is God's wrath). Their eschatology is not very sophisticated—it is sloppy. They don't recognize the clear chronological order of Revelation (chapters 1 to 11 in perfect chronological order and then chapters 12 to 22 in chronological order). They basically believe the seals, trumpets, and vials, are all happening at the same time with no real order to them. In reality—the seals come first, and then the trumpets and vials occur during God's wrath period (simultaneously).

1 Thessalonians 5:9

⁹ **For God hath not appointed us to wrath**, but to obtain salvation by our Lord Jesus Christ,

The first time the word tribulation is used in the book of Revelation is talking about a regenerated (regeneration referring to the new birth) believer (a child of God) literally going through tribulation. This is John on the Isle of Patmos:

Revelation 1:9

⁹ I John, who also am your brother, and
companion in tribulation, and in the kingdom
and patience of Jesus Christ, was in the isle that
is called Patmos, for the word of God, and for
the testimony of Jesus Christ.

The first time the word "tribulation' is referred to in
the entire New Testament is in Matthew chapter 13:

Matthew 13:20-21

²⁰ But he that received the seed into stony
places, the same is he that heareth the word,
and anon with joy receiveth it;

²¹ Yet hath he not root in himself, but dureth for
a while: for when **tribulation** or **persecution**
ariseth because of the word, by and by he is
offended.

A helpful tip on Biblical hermeneutics (Bible
interpretation) is to look at the first time a specific word is
used—and typically God will help us understand what that
word means. The word may be defined for us. This is the case
with the word "tribulation" here in Matthew 13. And it does
not refer to God's wrath—it refers to persecution. Matthew 13
is clearly teaching the reader that tribulation or persecution
can be the result of following the Word of God. Believers will
suffer persecution because of their faith in the Lord Jesus
Christ. Persecution or tribulation is what the world does to

believers. Tribulation (persecution) and wrath are clearly different. It is sloppy to argue they mean the same thing.

John was serving God and because of this, he was punished by being exiled to the Isle of Patmos. He was persecuted for his faith. He suffered tribulation—just like believers today suffer tribulation. 90% of the time we see the word "tribulation" in the New Testament—it is referring to God's people going through persecution for their faith and for serving the Lord. Tribulation is typically referring to persecution and affliction. Revelation 1:9 is not referring to the wrath of God being poured out on John on the Isle of Patmos. John was suffering persecution at the hands of the world—not at the hand of God. John is talking to fellow believers (the reader) in Revelation 1:9 assuring servants of Jesus Christ that they will be afflicted for their service to the Lord.

2 Timothy 3:12

[12] Yea, and all that will live godly in Christ Jesus shall suffer persecution.

Believers may not be appointed unto wrath—but we will suffer persecution for our faith in the Lord Jesus Christ. This is because there is a clear difference between tribulation and wrath. God's wrath does not come until after the great tribulation. This is after the sixth seal—and the rapture. Again—the order of events in the book of Revelation is: tribulation, rapture, wrath. Verse 17 of Revelation 6 (which occurs at the sixth seal when the sun and moon are darkened) states the great day of His wrath **IS** come:

Revelation 6:12-17

[12] And I beheld when he had opened the sixth seal, and, lo, there was a great earthquake; and **the sun became black as sackcloth of hair**, and the **moon became as blood**;

[13] And **the stars of heaven fell unto the earth**, even as a fig tree casteth her untimely figs, when she is shaken of a mighty wind.

[14] And the heaven departed as a scroll when it is rolled together; and every mountain and island were moved out of their places.

[15] And the kings of the earth, and the great men, and the rich men, and the chief captains, and the mighty men, and every bondman, and every free man, hid themselves in the dens and in the rocks of the mountains;

[16] And said to the mountains and rocks, Fall on us, and hide us from the face of him that sitteth on the throne, and from the wrath of the Lamb:

[17] **For the great day of his wrath is come; and who shall be able to stand?**

Verse 3 of Revelation 7 makes perfect sense when you understand the timeline of Revelation and end times in general (for example: the events we see laid out in Matthew 24):

Revelation 7:1-3

7 And after these things I saw four angels standing on the four corners of the earth, holding the four winds of the earth, that the wind should not blow on the earth, nor on the sea, nor on any tree.

[2] And I saw another angel ascending from the east, having the seal of the living God: and he cried with a loud voice to the four angels, to whom it was given to hurt the earth and the sea,

[3] Saying, Hurt not the earth, neither the sea, nor the trees, till we have sealed the servants of our God in their foreheads.

God's wrath has not yet started. The earth, sea, and the trees, have not yet been hurt. This makes sense when you understand the trumpets come after the seals. God's wrath has not yet been poured out prior to the sun and moon darkened, and the rapture. Once the 144,000 resurrected Israelites (chapter 3 has an extensive section on who the 144,000 are) are sealed (to act as a witness on the earth during God's wrath period), His wrath can begin. We see this same chronology in verse 15 of Revelation 15:

Revelation 15:1

15 And I saw another sign in heaven, great and marvellous, seven angels having the **seven last**

plagues; for in them is filled up **the wrath of God.**

When it comes to the seals, trumpets, and vials, try to remember them with this acronym: **STV**. We have 7 seals (S), 7 trumpets (T), and 7 vials (V).

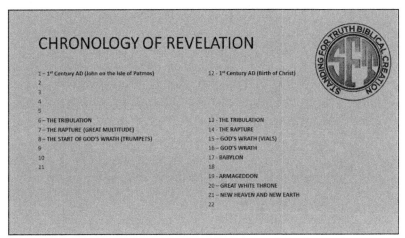

CHRONOLOGY OF REVELATION

1 – 1st Century AD (John on the Isle of Patmos)
2
3
4
5
6 – THE TRIBULATION
7 – THE RAPTURE (GREAT MULTITUDE)
8 – THE START OF GOD'S WRATH (TRUMPETS)
9
10
11

12 - 1st Century AD (Birth of Christ)
13 - THE TRIBULATION
14 - THE RAPTURE
15 – GOD'S WRATH (VIALS)
16 – GOD'S WRATH
17 - BABYLON
18
19 - ARMAGEDDON
20 – GREAT WHITE THRONE
21 – NEW HEAVEN AND NEW EARTH
22

Revelation chronology chart made by this author to help the reader visualize the points made in this chapter pertaining to the structural nature of the book of Revelation.

THE WRATH OF THE LAMB

I have pointed to the consistent correlation between Matthew 24 and Revelation 6. Both chapters describe the sun and moon being darkened. These cosmological disturbances occur after the tribulation, and before God's wrath. We also find the elect being gathered after the sun and moon go dark in Matthew 24, and a great multitude that no man could number instantaneously appearing in heaven in Revelation 7. This occurs after the sun and moon go dark in Revelation 6.

Pre-tribulation rapturists have attempted to reject this perfect correlation by claiming Jesus Christ is not found in Revelation 6. They argue this is a different cosmological event than in Matthew 24. This is flabbergasting. The Lamb (Jesus Christ) is most definitely present in Revelation 6—and He is present after the sun and moon go dark—before God pours out His wrath:

Revelation 6:16-17

16 And said to the mountains and rocks, Fall on us, and hide us from **the face of him that sitteth on the throne**, and from **the wrath of the Lamb**:

17 For the great day of his wrath is come; and who shall be able to stand?

Notice the emphasized words in verse 16 of Revelation 6. Unbelievers (those not caught up at the rapture) are in fear as they see *"the face of him that sitteth on the throne."* The Lamb is present in this passage because this passage is describing the predicted cosmological disturbances that would occur right before Jesus Christ comes in the clouds to rapture His elect. There has been no convincing counter to the consistent correlation between Matthew 24, Revelation 6, and Revelation 7 (the great multitude).

CHAPTER TWO

DANIEL'S 70 WEEKS

The book of Daniel is an amazing book that contains several incredible prophecies. Firstly—we need to understand how to rightly divide this significant book (much like how we rightly divide the book of Revelation). An example of rightly dividing the scriptures is by knowing the difference between passages that are symbolic or figurative, and passages that are literal. We also need to understand that some things written in God's word are being spoken by God and other things are being spoken by human beings (which means they could be saying things that are not necessarily 100% truthful).

When it comes to Old Testament Bible prophecy—it is very important that we rightly divide between events that have already happened—and events that will happen in the future. A prime example of what I mean by this is the book of Revelation. The majority of the book of Revelation is describing events that are going to occur in the future. It becomes more difficult to tell the difference between that which has already occurred, and that which will occur when reading the book of Daniel. But by studying this amazing book—we can begin to figure these things out. This will be part of what I will be focusing on in this valuable chapter on Bible prophecy.

The book of Daniel is similar to the book of Revelation in how it is structured. Daniel is structured in 2 sections. You can basically cut the book right down the middle with chapters 1 through 6 comprising mostly stories. These are some very well-known Bible stories. For example—this is where we read about Daniel and his friends standing up for the truth and standing up for that which is right. This amazing book contains an abundance of important life lessons. And these lessons are especially significant when it comes to the last days. We as Christians are to stand up against evil no matter what. We are called to remain faithful and put our trust in the Lord. God will get us through troubling times. It is God who gives us strength.

The story of Shadrach, Meshach, and Abednego is found in these opening chapters. This is the famous story where they are thrown into the fiery furnace. We also see the famous story of Daniel being thrown into the Lion's den in these opening chapters. These are stories that have helped millions of Christians get through tough times. They are true stories and real historical events that teach believers how to fight through tribulation and persecution. We as Christians will go through hard times, and it's stories like the ones found in the book of Daniel that keep us strong and faithful. Many aspects of this book help to prepare believers for trials and troubles. A major feature of Daniel's 70th week is tribulation, and the book of Daniel will prepare Christians for the types of challenging times we will face in the last days. We need to learn to stand firm now in order to stand firm when persecution arises—the type of persecution that will be endured during the great tribulation.

Chapters 7–12 of Daniel is where we find some of the most technical and amazing prophecies in the entire Bible. These latter chapters of Daniel hold some extremely heavy Bible prophecy. When you study these remarkable prophecies deeply—you understand just how exciting and fascinating this book is.

Let's start with some context and background before we begin to examine some of the deeper passages found in Daniel. The book of Daniel is being written while the Jews are being held captive in Babylon. The first temple has been destroyed, the nation of Judah has been decimated, and the Jews have been scattered into all nations, with many being held captive.

Chapter 2 of Daniel describes the well-known great image. This great image has a head of gold, chest and arms of silver, loins of brass, legs of iron, and feet of iron mingled with clay.

Daniel 2:31-35

³¹ Thou, O king, sawest, and behold **a great image**. This great image, whose brightness was excellent, stood before thee; and the form thereof was terrible.

³²**This image's head was of fine gold, his breast and his arms of silver, his belly and his thighs of brass,**

³³**His legs of iron, his feet part of iron and part of clay.**

³⁴ Thou sawest till that a stone was cut out without hands, which smote the image upon his feet that were of iron and clay, and brake them to pieces.

³⁵ Then was the iron, the clay, the brass, the silver, and the gold, broken to pieces together, and became like the chaff of the summer threshingfloors; and the wind carried them away, that no place was found for them: and the stone that smote the image became a great mountain, and filled the whole earth.

This is a great image that has been talked and written about extensively. It has invoked remarkable discussion and debate. The aspects of this great image represent **4 great kingdoms**. The head of gold represents **Babylon**. The chest and arms of silver symbolize the **Medo-Persian empire**. The brass represents **Grecia**, and the **Roman Empire** is the fourth great kingdom. These 4 great kingdoms are mentioned repeatedly in the book of Daniel, and they have an important application for end times theology.

Daniel 7 is where we get the same 4 aspects of the great image, except in this instance they are represented as 4 great beasts. The first beast is a lion (Babylon). The bear is the second beast (Medo-Persian empire). The third beast—which is a Leopard—represents the kingdom of Greece, and the final beast represents the Roman Empire. The fourth beast is described as strong and terrible—and more powerful than all the beasts before it.

Daniel 7:2-9

² Daniel spake and said, I saw in my vision by night, and, behold, the four winds of the heaven strove upon the great sea.

³ And **four great beasts came up from the sea, diverse one from another.**

⁴ The first was like **a lion**, and had eagle's wings: I beheld till the wings thereof were plucked, and it was lifted up from the earth, and made stand upon the feet as a man, and a man's heart was given to it.

⁵ And behold another beast, a second, like to **a bear**, and it raised up itself on one side, and it had three ribs in the mouth of it between the teeth of it: and they said thus unto it, Arise, devour much flesh.

⁶ After this I beheld, and lo another, like **a leopard**, which had upon the back of it four wings of a fowl; the beast had also four heads; and dominion was given to it.

⁷ After this I saw in the night visions, and behold a fourth beast**, dreadful and terrible**, and **strong exceedingly**; and it had **great iron teeth**: it devoured and brake in pieces, and stamped the residue with the feet of it: and it was diverse from all the beasts that were before it; and it had ten horns.

⁸ I considered the horns, and, **behold, there came up among them another little horn, before whom there were three of the first horns plucked up by the roots: and, behold, in this horn were eyes like the eyes of man, and a mouth speaking great things.**

⁹ I beheld till the thrones were cast down, and the Ancient of days did sit, whose garment was white as snow, and the hair of his head like the pure wool: his throne was like the fiery flame, and his wheels as burning fire.

In verse 8—we read about a little horn that came out of this beast (the fourth beast). The description of this little horn fits that of a man. We see this in Revelation 13:

Revelation 13

13 And I stood upon the sand of the sea, and saw **a beast rise up** out of the sea, having seven heads and ten horns, and upon his horns ten crowns, and upon his heads the name of blasphemy.

²And the beast which I saw was like unto a leopard, and his feet were as the feet of a bear, and his mouth as the mouth of a lion: and the dragon gave him his power, and his seat, and great authority.

³And I saw one of his heads as it were wounded to death; and his deadly wound was healed: and all the world wondered after the beast.

⁴ And they worshipped the dragon which gave power unto the beast: and they worshipped the beast, saying, Who is like unto the beast? **who is able to make war with him?**

⁵ And there was given unto him a mouth speaking great things and blasphemies; and power was given unto him to continue forty and two months.

⁶ And he opened his mouth in blasphemy against God, to blaspheme his name, and his tabernacle, and them that dwell in heaven.

The little horn described in Daniel 7 is in fact the Antichrist depicted in Revelation 13. Verse 4 of Revelation 13 describes the Antichrist as having a mouth speaking great things and blasphemies. It also informs us he will continue in power for forty and two months (42 months/3.5 years). Compare this to verse 8 of Daniel 7:

Daniel 7:8

⁸ I considered the horns, and, behold, there came up among them another **little horn**, before whom there were three of the first horns plucked up by the roots: and, **behold, in this horn were eyes like the eyes of man, and a mouth speaking great things.**

53

The little horn of Daniel 7 is depicted as speaking great things in the same way the Antichrist of Revelation 13 is. Let us examine verses 19-25 of Daniel 7:

Daniel 7:19-25

[19] Then I would know **the truth of the fourth beast**, which was **diverse from all the others**, **exceeding dreadful, whose teeth were of iron**, **and his nails of brass**; **which devoured, brake in pieces, and stamped the residue with his feet;**

[20] And of the ten horns that were in his head, and of the other which came up, and before whom three fell; even of that horn that had eyes, and **a mouth that spake very great things**, **whose look was more stout than his fellows.**

[21] I beheld, and **the same horn made war with the saints, and prevailed against them;**

[22] Until the Ancient of days came, and judgment was given to the saints of the most High; and the time came that the saints possessed the kingdom.

[23] Thus he said, **The fourth beast shall be the fourth kingdom upon earth, which shall be diverse from all kingdoms, and shall devour the whole earth, and shall tread it down, and break it in pieces.**

²⁴ And the ten horns out of this kingdom are ten kings that shall arise: and another shall rise after them; and he shall be diverse from the first, and he shall subdue three kings.

²⁵ And **he shall speak great words against the most High, and shall wear out the saints of the most High, and think to change times and laws: and they shall be given into his hand until a time and times and the dividing of time.**

When reading these verses—they should sound very familiar. They sound almost exactly like the verses found in Revelation 13—which describe the reign of the Antichrist. The Antichrist is described as making war with the saints, and even overcoming them. The saints refer to believers—those that are saved. This tells us the great tribulation period has to do with believers, and the final war (advanced by the Antichrist, the false prophet, and the dragon) against them. Both Daniel 7 and Revelation 13 make it clear that the Antichrist will make war against the saints and overcome them. The Antichrist is given power over all tongues and nations. This is essentially describing a one world government. This is the New World Order that the Antichrist will rule over. He will be the leader of this final kingdom. And he will use his power to fight Christians. Verse 25 of Daniel 9 provides a specific amount of time the Antichrist will continue in power (just like we see in Revelation 13). This time is described as **"time and times and the dividing of time."** What does this mean? A time is one, times are two, and the dividing of time is half of one (0.5). This period is 3.5

years—or 42 months (as provided in Revelation 13). These similarities are intriguing. 42 months and "time and times and the dividing of time" is the same. We are being provided significant details of events in the last days. Historicists that want to argue these are years rather than days are refuted by the fact that we have both 3.5 years *and* 42 months. We are given days, years, *and* months. These details are obviously meant to be understood literally.

Daniel is provided information on 4 extremely powerful kingdoms: Babylon, Medo-Persia, Grecia, and Rome. The fourth beast is Rome (a fulfilled prophecy), but also represents the final worldwide kingdom—the global government—or New World Order (which the Antichrist will be ruler of). This is where dual-prophecy fulfillment comes into play (which I will cover in great detail later in this chapter).

Jesus Christ came to this earth the first time during the fourth kingdom—Rome. It was at this time that Jesus conquered spiritually. He will come again during the fourth kingdom—but in its future end times representation. We know this based on the incredible similarities between the books of Daniel and Revelation. *Jesus came during the Roman empire—and His second coming will be during the worldwide empire.* Remember—the little horn of Daniel 7 does all the things the Antichrist does—and he does it for 3.5 years—which is 42 months. The Antichrist will be in power over this one world government when Jesus Christ comes the second time. This time He will conquer physically. The first coming was a spiritual conquering, and the second coming will be a physical victory where the Antichrist, false prophet, and Satan (the false trinity) are destroyed, and His millennial kingdom will be set up.

THE MESSIAH

Daniel chapter 9 verses 24-27 are some of the most discussed verses of all time. Countless books and endless sermons have been done on these fascinating verses. There are many different opinions pertaining to the meaning of these verses. I want to provide the reader with some amazing insight into what Daniel 9:24-27 is saying—especially as it relates to end times Bible prophecy:

Daniel 9:24-27

[24] Seventy weeks are determined upon thy people and upon thy holy city, to finish the transgression, and to make an end of sins, and to make reconciliation for iniquity, and to bring in everlasting righteousness, and to seal up the vision and prophecy, and to anoint the most Holy.

[25] Know therefore and understand, that from the going forth of the commandment to restore and to build Jerusalem unto the Messiah the Prince shall be seven weeks, and threescore and two weeks: the street shall be built again, and the wall, even in troublous times.

^{26} And after threescore and two weeks shall Messiah be cut off, but not for himself: and the people of the prince that shall come shall destroy the city and the sanctuary; and the end thereof shall be with a flood, and unto the end of the war desolations are determined.

^{27} And he shall confirm the covenant with many for one week: and in the midst of the week he shall cause the sacrifice and the oblation to cease, and for the overspreading of abominations he shall make it desolate, even until the consummation, and that determined shall be poured upon the desolate.

These are 4 very technical, and remarkable passages. Firstly—I want to simplify these verses into what we definitely know, and by taking this effective approach, we will be able to fill in what at first may have appeared unknown.

At the beginning of Daniel 9, Daniel was studying the 70 years of Babylonian captivity. Now we see Daniel receiving a different prophecy—a prophecy of 70 weeks. These weeks are not typical weeks (7 days in a week). These are weeks of years (groups of 7 years rather than 7 days). We are dealing with 70 weeks that are 70 periods of 7 years each.

Now that the 70 years of Babylonian captivity has been understood—we have 70 weeks that are going to accomplish some very important things. These 70 weeks will accomplish:

- Finishing the transgression,

- Making an end of sins,

- Reconciliation for iniquity,

- Bringing in everlasting righteousness,

- Sealing up the vision and prophecy,

- The anointing of the most Holy.

Out of these important things that will be accomplished in the 70 weeks of time, there are many things that we know. We know the context is dealing with Jerusalem and the Jews.

How do we make an end of sins and make reconciliation for iniquity? This obviously does not mean that everybody is going to stop sinning. What this is dealing with is the coming of Jesus Christ. Jesus died on the cross for the sins of the world. He paid for our sins. By Jesus' death, burial, and resurrection, He has made an end of sins. He has also made reconciliation for iniquity. As the reader can already see—Daniel 9 is an amazing and undeniable fulfilled prophecy of the coming of Jesus Christ (and what He accomplished on the cross).

Isaiah 53:5-6

[5] But **he was wounded for our transgressions, he was bruised for our iniquities**: **the**

chastisement of our peace was upon him; and **with his stripes we are healed.**

[6] All we like sheep have gone astray; we have turned every one to his own way; and **the Lord hath laid on him the iniquity of us all.**

Believers are saved by the righteousness of Jesus Christ. It is not by our own righteousness that we are saved. Our righteousness is like filthy rags. It is by the righteousness of Jesus Christ that we are justified, regenerated and one day glorified. It is by the righteousness of God through faith in the finished work of Jesus Christ that we have salvation. Jesus Christ brought in **everlasting righteousness**. The righteousness of Jesus Christ that is imputed unto believers is everlasting righteousness. When a person trusts Christ for salvation, they receive everlasting life. *A believer is justified, regenerated, and predestined for glorification.* The iniquities and transgressions of believers have been forgiven. Believers have been reconciled to God by the blood of Jesus Christ.

What do we know so far? This prophecy has to do with Jesus Christ and His death, burial, and resurrection (which brought in everlasting righteousness and made an end of sins). This is all very clear. Verse 24 of Daniel 9 is clearly referring to Jesus Christ—The Messiah.

The Jews were looking for the Messiah as someone who would be a great and mighty King, a King of Israel that would lead them back into their former triumph. But Messiah is actually cut off—and this cutting off is not for Himself, but for the world. The Messiah is cut off for you, me, and for everybody. He was bruised for our iniquities and wounded for our transgressions. The Lord hath laid on Him the iniquity of us all. This is not what the Jews were expecting.

Finishing the transgression is also mentioned. This seems to indicate that there exists some type of wickedness that is not yet finished—but will be finished during the 70 weeks. We also see that the vision and prophecy will be sealed up. This is basically the tying up of loose ends for Bible prophecies and visions. There are many important prophecies that need to come to pass, and these 70 weeks will complete those. These 70 weeks will fulfill those prophecies and visions.

To anoint the most Holy is a reference to Jesus Christ. Jesus is the most Holy—and He is the anointed. We know the word *"Christ"* is the Greek word for the Hebrew word *"Messiah"*. We also know that both *"Christ"* and *"Messiah"* mean ***anointed.***

All throughout the Old Testament—priests and kings were anointed. Anointment is basically where we get our word "ointment" from. Priests and kings were anointed with oil in the Old Testament. Jesus Christ is *Prophet*, *Priest*, and *King*. Although priests and kings were anointed, Jesus Christ has a triple anointing. Jesus is the prophet that Moses prophesied would come. He is the son of David who will sit on the throne of His father David (anointed as King). He is also a Priest forever at the order of Melchisedec (**Hebrews 7:17**).

Considering everything discussed so far—it's absolutely clear that verse 24 is describing Jesus Christ.

61

In verse 25 of Daniel 9—The Messiah (Jesus Christ) is being called Prince. And we know Jesus is referred to as the Prince of peace. We also see in verse 25, 69 weeks mentioned (7 weeks and 62 weeks). It is very important that we don't just combine the 7 and 62 weeks into a single 69-week consecutive period. No—these are 2 components that equal 69 weeks (7 and 62). The passage clearly states that there will be 7 weeks—and then after the 7 weeks—there will be 62 weeks. We see an obvious gap between the 7th week and the 8th week. This is made evident by the 2-component nature of the 7 and 62 weeks. We will also discuss the gap between the 69 and 70 weeks later in this chapter.

This reality of a gap between the 7th and the 8th week is important to note for many reasons, and an additional reason is based on the preterist argument that asserts there is no gap between the 69th and 70th week. But wait a minute—*the 70 weeks are broken up into 3 components*—and there exists a clear gap between the 7th and 8th weeks and between the 69th and 70th weeks. *God broke the 70 weeks up into 3 elements—not us.* The preterists need to read these verses more clearly. If the preterist would read these verses carefully, without any preconceived ideas, they will see that we have 7 weeks, then a gap, 62 weeks, and then another gap. This means that these weeks come in 3 phases—and not 2. I have even seen those within my own eschatological camp (pre-wrath) make the mistake of only thinking the 70 weeks is made of 2 phases. When we study verse 25 meticulously—we can only conclude that there exist 3 phases. The phases are: 7 weeks, 62 weeks, and then 1 week (Daniel's 70th week).

Verse 25 also refers to Cyrus making the great commandment to build the temple and Jerusalem—and sending the Jews back to their land. Jerusalem, the street, and the wall around it will be rebuilt in the promised land. This will be done in troublesome times.

It is in verse 26 that we read about The Messiah (Jesus Christ) being cut off. This occurs after the 69 weeks (therefore after the first 2 phases—the 7 and 62 weeks). Cut off refers to being killed. Jesus Christ was cut off (He died) for the world. He was not cut off for Himself. As I said earlier: *the Jews were looking for the Messiah as being a great and mighty King—a King of Israel that would lead them back into their former triumph. But Messiah is actually cut off and not for Himself, but for the world—for you, for me, for everybody. He was bruised for our iniquities and wounded for our transgressions. The Lord hath laid on Him the iniquity of us all.* Again—this is a beautiful—and undeniable fulfilled prophecy of our Lord and Savior Jesus Christ. Jesus died for the sins of the whole world. **All who believe and trust in Him will have everlasting life—and never come into condemnation.**

The reader may be wondering a few things about the 7 weeks and the 62 weeks—especially if they've been taught that the 7 and 62 weeks make for 1 phase—and not 2. Because we today have what's called hindsight—many people have erroneously looked to when the Messiah was cut off (since we know today when this happened), which was roughly 33 AD. AD refers to after the birth of Jesus Christ, and BC refers to time before the birth of Jesus. Since Jesus was about 33 and a half years old when He was cut off (died for our sins), Bible

63

scholars have attempted to work their way backwards to where they can say this verse was telling them exactly when Jesus Christ would die on the cross. They start with 33 AD and work their way backwards by adding the 69 weeks (69x7), and calculating their way back to the prophecy. But unfortunately, this hasn't worked smoothly. These calculations do not effectively go back to when the pronouncement was made. We do not get a clear backwards calculation to when the commandment was given to restore and rebuild Jerusalem. What we end up getting from those that don't see the gap between the 7th and 8th weeks is a lot of tweaking of the numbers. Basically—these Bible scholars play around with the numbers until they get the date that they want. But it just comes across as sloppy and unconvincing. The reason the calculations are unconvincing, and require a lot of adjusting, is because there is a gap. Since we have the advantage of retrospection—we can essentially modify the numbers enough to where we get an answer that seems right, or the answer we want.

If there isn't a gap, and the Bible is actually telling us exactly how many years until Jesus Christ dies on the cross—then we would expect numerous faithful believers (including the disciples and apostles) to have figured out that basic math. These calculations are uncomplicated, and should work out efficiently to the point where believers at the time of Jesus Christ's death would acknowledge this. Why don't these numbers add up perfectly? It's because there is a gap. There are 2 gaps (a gap between the 7th and 8th weeks, and a gap between the 69th and 70th weeks). Remember—we have 3 phases or components. We have 7 weeks, 62 weeks, and then

1 week. It's not just 70 weeks. No—it's 7 weeks, 62 weeks, and 1 week. *There are 3 elements to Daniel's 70 weeks.* We need to understand this—which is why I am spending a lot of time on this topic. I want the reader to be well equipped to not only refute the pre-tribulation rapture, but also to refute preterism (full and partial).

The gap between the 7 weeks and the 62 weeks makes tremendous sense. This is because God did not want them to know the exact day and hour Jesus Christ would be cut off. This would be giving the Jews far too much information. When too much information is provided in Biblical prophecy—it becomes what is called a **self-fulfilling prophecy.**

Daniel 9 is explicit. God wants us to know that there are going to be 70 weeks of prophecy. These weeks are significant and will bring about a number of necessary events.

The 7 years is referring to the temple, wall, and street being rebuilt. When Cyrus gave a pronouncement—it makes complete sense that this phase of rebuilding would take about 49 years. A 49-year component of Daniel's 70 weeks is most likely referring to the Jews making their way back to Jerusalem and getting the temple (plus the street and wall) rebuilt. This means that the 7 weeks ends with the temple, wall, and the street being rebuilt. This ends element 1 of the 70 weeks. Then we have the 62 weeks (phase 2/element 2) ending with Jesus Christ being cut off for the world.

DEBUNKING PRETERISM

There is no reasonable way to believe in preterism today. If we were to just forget the arguments employed by preterists for one second—and simply look at the way the world is—we can make no other conclusion than to say the prophecies of Daniel, and the book of Revelation, are coming true. This world is not getting better. The stage is set for a one world government and a one world leader. We already have the technology available for a one world currency. And we know there are religious leaders in the world working towards a one world religion. Preterists are incapable of addressing this reality.

The fact that I am even writing this book—and taking time to dismantle preterist arguments—is proof that preterism is false. This means that Jesus has not yet come back—even though preterists want to say the second coming of Jesus Christ was in 70 AD. It doesn't take very long to settle this debate. Debating whether or not Jesus has already returned—and if the book of Revelation has been fulfilled—is essentially tantamount to debating if aliens exist—or if the moon is made of green cheese. Of course, Jesus has not come back yet. And what we see prophesied in Revelation is coming to pass all around us. Therefore, preterists can make careers out of twisting the scripture all the way—but both God's Word and the world's current situation is irrefutable evidence against the position that says most, or all, of Biblical prophecy has been fulfilled. This is a ludicrous position that is simply not defensible. It is even challenging to take seriously.

We have not yet been resurrected. We do not currently have glorified bodies. The wicked have not been destroyed—but they will be destroyed—in the future. Preterists are forced to spiritualize everything to justify their position. But the Bible is clear when it says we will be raised from corruptible to incorruptible. I want the reader to ask themselves if they have a perfect and sinless glorified body? The answer is an obvious no. We are living in a fallen world, and are still under the curse that was brought upon this world when Adam and Eve sinned in the garden. Preterism is dangerous because it results in a denial of important Biblical teachings.

The Bible says that death will be defeated. There will be no more death in the new heavens and new earth. Death still exists today. If this is as good as it's going to get—that is sad. We see death, disease, sadness, tragedy, and so many more things that will not be present in the new heavens and new earth—but full preterists want to say that *THIS IS* the new heavens and new earth. This is heresy. We are not in the new heavens and new earth, and the lion is not lying down with the lamb. We see human death—and animal death. But this will not be the case when death is trounced. The dead have not been judged and Satan is still deceiving the nations.

Preterism (partial and full) is completely unbiblical and unreasonable. It is a position that cannot be rationalized. Try telling people in other countries who are suffering from war and starvation, that they are currently living in the new heavens and new earth and are ultimately in paradise. Or try telling those who have lost loved ones in hurricanes, wildfires, and other horrible natural disasters, that this is paradise—and this is as good as it's going to get. Let's see the response from those who have suffered greatly from the horrors of war when a preterist tells them we are living in the time of universal peace!

The first coming of Jesus Christ was literal. He existed physically and literally on this planet. This was a fulfillment of the Old Testament prophecies. Acts 1 tells us that Jesus Christ will return in the same way as he left—in the clouds. I covered this in chapter 1. Has Jesus Christ come back in the clouds for every eye to see Him? No, He hasn't. But He will!

The current heavens and earth will be destroyed by fire. The elements will dissolve:

2 Peter 3:10-12

[10] But the day of the Lord will come as a thief in the night; <u>in the which the heavens shall pass away with a great noise</u>, and the <u>elements shall melt with fervent heat, the earth also</u> and the works that are therein shall be burned up.

[11] Seeing then that all these things shall be dissolved, what manner of persons ought ye to be in all holy conversation and godliness,

[12] Looking for and hasting unto the coming of the day of God, <u>wherein the heavens being on fire shall be dissolved, and the elements shall melt with fervent heat?</u>

Do these verses sound like they could apply to the destruction of the Jewish temple in 70 AD? Definitely not! This has not happened yet.

The Bible is clear: there will be scoffers in the last days asking (in a mocking way) where is the second coming of Jesus Christ?

2 Peter 3:1-8

3 This second epistle, beloved, I now write unto you; in both which I stir up your pure minds by way of remembrance:

² That ye may be mindful of the words which were spoken before by the holy prophets, and of the commandment of us the apostles of the Lord and Saviour:

³ **Knowing this first, <u>that there shall come in the last days scoffers</u>, walking after their own lusts,**

⁴ And saying, **<u>Where is the promise of his coming? for since the fathers fell asleep, all things continue as they were from the beginning of the creation.</u>**

⁵ For this they willingly are ignorant of, that by the word of God the heavens were of old, and the earth standing out of the water and in the water:

6 Whereby the world that then was, being overflowed with water, perished:

7 But the heavens and the earth, which are now, by the same word are kept in store, reserved unto fire against the day of judgment and perdition of ungodly men.

8 But, beloved, be not ignorant of this one thing, that **one day is with the Lord as a thousand years, and a thousand years as one day.**

If Jesus really did come back in 70 AD, Peter's words here would make no sense. The reason there are scoffers today asking *"where is the promise of His coming?"* is because it has been over 2000 years since His first coming. If Jesus came back 40 years after His death, burial and resurrection, then this would have been a quick return. Many, including preterists (which is why many argue for a second coming in 70 AD) believe there is a delay in the second coming, but there is no delay. Verse 8 of 2 Peter 3 makes it clear that to God one day is as a thousand years, and a thousand years as one day. God has a different calendar. He's already been to our funeral. 2000 years to humans is not the same as to God.

The objective reader has already seen throughout this book (up to this point) several instances of why preterism is a false doctrine. I want to continue refuting preterism and show the reader more reasons why it makes no sense to say that "everything has already happened" or even "most of these prophecies have already happened". An important aspect of

Bible prophecy to understand is called **Dual Prophecy Fulfillment.**

When it comes to Bible prophecy—there is what's called an immediate fulfillment (for back when the prophecy was made) and then also a great—and more literal, or dramatic fulfillment for the future.

In other words—we have both an immediate application and a future application. This is found all throughout the Bible literally from Genesis to Revelation. Prophecies in the Old Testament have a dual, and triple fulfillment. The reason for this is because the prophecy has an application for the generation back then and also applications for future generations. The ultimate application is fulfilled in its end times application. The world goes through cycles and because of this we have prophetic cycles.

This all applies to Daniel's 70th week. Preterists claim there is no future 7-year period. They argue the 70th week of Daniel was all fulfilled in the past (during Jesus Christ's ministry, death, and in 70 AD with the destruction of the temple). This is where they go wrong—they don't understand dual prophecy fulfillment. Not only that—but many of the aspects in these significant Bible prophecies have not literally occurred. Unfortunately—preterists must accuse the Bible of some very serious exaggerations.

Yes—you could argue that Jesus was anointed with the Holy Spirit at His Baptism—and you could even say that He's ruling and reigning in our hearts today (for believers). Remember—those that are regenerated have the righteousness of Christ by faith. This means that Jesus Christ is reigning right now—that is—in the hearts of justified believers. But preterists want to take this one false step further by claiming this reality is the literal 1000-year millennial reign. They must forget that this world is a mess. This world has degenerated and devolved. Morality is being thrown out the window. This world is clearly not getting any better (until Jesus Christ returns). We are just one step away from a new world order and a one world currency. The stage is all set for the arrival of the Antichrist. World War 1 saw the league of nations, World War 2 witnessed the creation of the United Nations (the embryonic one world government), and there is a good chance the next world war (World War 3) will see the creation of the beast (new world order). Again—this world is not getting any better. You'd literally have to be living under a rock to not see that there is a war for the world.

Is Jesus really ruling and reigning physically on this earth? Of course not. But He will rule and reign on this earth (physically and literally) one day (Revelation 20). The devil is called the god of this world. Satan roams the earth seeking whom he may devour **(1 Peter 5:8)**. Satan is deceiving the nations. One day Satan will be bound in hell for 1000 years, and then eventually thrown into the lake of fire. This has not yet happened, and to say it has is absurd. The Bible talks clearly about the rulers of the darkness of this world. It talks about spiritual wickedness in high places.

Jesus Christ is ruling in the hearts of the elect (believers). Yes—this is true. But He will one day *literally* come back to this earth where He will rule and reign with a rod of iron. If preterists understood shadow fulfillments with an eventually literal, or more dramatic fulfillment, they wouldn't fall into these bizarre interpretations.

Jesus Christ will one day be anointed. This will be a literal anointing. He will have oil poured on His head (exactly what we have seen practiced in the Old Testament with prophets, kings, and priests). We have a shadow fulfillment with much of what has been talked about in Daniel 9—but we have definitely not had the literal and more dramatic fulfillments (which will be fulfilled at the Millennium).

EXAMPLES OF DUAL-PROPHECY FULFILLMENT

Preterism and historicism are both false—and do not recognize the cyclical nature of world events and Bible prophecies. There is nothing new under the sun—and there have been numerous partial or shadow fulfillments—but this does not negate a future more literal and dramatic fulfillment. Futurists recognize the signs and the times. It does not take much to see that this world is heading into a state that has been predicted thousands of years ago in both Daniel and Revelation. In 2022 (the writing of this book) it is ridiculous to claim these events predicted in scripture have all already taken place—and there is nothing for the future. To be blunt—it's difficult to take these various preterist positions seriously. If we were a 1000 or more years into the past—the preterists or historicists may have had an easier time making their case—but today—in 2022—it's impossible to make a convincing case for these positions since we can literally see

Bible prophecy being fulfilled around us. Preterists essentially must argue that the coming great reset, one world government, one world currency, and one world leader, is just a coincidence—or some may simply be forced to deny reality.

A lot of what is described in Daniel has happened, and it will happen again (but on a far greater scale). Preterists don't understand this. Or they pretend not to. Remember—the Bible is replete with examples of dual and triple prophecy fulfillment. In this section—I want to go over just a few of the numerous Biblical examples of dual fulfillment.

The day of the Lord is an example of dual and triple prophecy fulfillment that not even preterists can ignore. How many "mini" days of the Lord do we see throughout the scriptures? A lot. We frequently read about the day of the Lord being "at hand". This means it's about to happen. If the day of the Lord is about to happen in the past—and also talked about as coming in the future—then what we have are many foreshadows of the main day of the Lord. We see numerous small-scale days of the Lord in the Old Testament that had an immediate occurrence—but the immediate occurrence was ultimately a foreshadowing of the main event in the future. The problem with the preterist understanding is their inability to recognize the fact that shadow fulfillments are not the exact fulfillment. A line of evidential support for this can be seen simply by reading these Old Testament day of the Lord passages—and realizing the descriptions of them appear exaggerated—since their Old Testament occurrence was not exactly as the Prophet said it would be. The reason these descriptions appear exaggerated is because they are only "appetizers". The main course is not until the future. The more dramatic day of the Lord is still in the future. Preterists take partial or shadow fulfillments and argue these are the literal dramatic fulfillments. As a result—they accuse the Bible of extreme exaggeration. They essentially make the Prophets look like they aren't getting all the major details right. No—the Prophets got the details correct—but the Preterists don't understand that the major details are going to be fulfilled in the future.

Another great and easy to recognize example of this is found with the destruction of Babylon in Jeremiah 50 and 51:

Jeremiah 51:64

[64] And thou shalt say, Thus shall Babylon sink, and shall not rise from the evil that I will bring upon her: and they shall be weary. Thus far are the words of Jeremiah.

Much of the details provided in Jeremiah 50 and 51 about the destruction of Babylon are for the future destruction of Babylon (Revelation 18). To take every detail in these chapters and force them into their immediate fulfillment is to ignore the clear shadow fulfillment versus future exact fulfillment being revealed.

The Medes and the Persians defeated Babylon (immediate fulfillment). But this immediate fulfillment or application did not occur precisely the way described in Jeremiah 50 and 51. The destruction of Babylon meant the replacement of Babylon as the most powerful kingdom at that time. Remember—it went: Babylon, Medo-Persia, Grecia, and then Rome.

There are certain aspects of these chapters in Jeremiah that did not occur with the defeat of Babylon. This is because there is another future fulfillment. This is obvious since Revelation was written long after Jeremiah. Babylon was destroyed in the Old Testament (there is much debate about who modern-day Babylon is), and Revelation (talking about events in the future) describes another destruction of Babylon. And this second and more dramatic destruction of Babylon will comprise every detail provided in the Old Testament. This is when the partial fulfillment becomes an exact fulfillment. Again—you can't go into studying end times theology without this basic knowledge (this is why preterists are incredibly sloppy in their Bible interpretation on this topic).

Revelation 18:1-3

18 And after these things I saw another angel come down from heaven, having great power; and the earth was lightened with his glory.

² And he cried mightily with a strong voice, saying, **Babylon the great is fallen, is fallen, and is become the habitation of devils, and the hold of every foul spirit, and a cage of every unclean and hateful bird.**

³ **For all nations have drunk of the wine of the wrath of her fornication, and the kings of the earth have committed fornication with**

**her, and the merchants of the earth are
waxed rich through the abundance of her
delicacies.**

Although Babylon fell in Jeremiah 50 and 51—there remains a future Babylon that will be wiped out. If this weren't the case—Revelation 18 would make no sense. The future fulfillment is parallel with the above verses in Revelation 18. We find many parallels between Jeremiah 50, 51 and Revelation 18. This is because much of what is found in chapters 50 and 51 of Jeremiah is for the future (which we read about in Revelation 18). Many aspects of these prophecies are fulfilled during their immediate context—but **ALL will be fulfilled in its future application.**

We find an amazing example of dual prophecy in chapter 22 of Genesis:

Genesis 22:8-9

[8] And Abraham said, **My son, God will provide himself a lamb for a burnt offering**: so they went both of them together.

[9] And they came to the place which God had told him of; and Abraham built an altar there, and laid the wood in order, and bound Isaac his son, and laid him on the altar upon the wood.

This is the story of Abraham offering up his son on the altar. Abraham prophesied that God would provide **Himself a lamb** (Jesus Christ). After Abraham was prevented from offering up his son—a ram was provided as a sacrifice. In this immediate occurrence—a ram was provided—but not a lamb. The lamb (Jesus Christ—God manifest in the flesh) is for the future—and when Jesus died for the sins of the world—this prophecy was fulfilled in all its amazing details. The ram is different from the lamb, and the sacrificing of the ram is a partial fulfillment of the main event with Jesus Christ being provided as a sacrifice for the whole world. Jesus Christ is the real Lamb of God that takes away the sins of the world. In the immediate context—a literal animal (ram) is provided—but in the future (at the time of Christ) we have the exact fulfillment. Preterists basically look at the shadow fulfillment (a ram being offered) as being "close enough". No—a ram is not close enough. Now—preterists will most likely concede that yes this is a dual-prophecy fulfillment—but then completely ignore the dual and triple prophecy fulfillments when it comes to end times. It really is mind boggling.

In this specific example found in Genesis, a ram still achieved the same purpose. It filled the same void. But the prophecy itself lets us know that there is still something for the future. And this lamb ends up being Jesus Christ—the Lamb of God.

Jonah is another excellent example of dual-prophecy fulfillment. Jonah talks about being in the ocean—but then speaks about being in hell:

Jonah 2

2 Then Jonah prayed unto the Lord his God out of **the fish's belly**,

² And said, I cried by reason of mine affliction unto the Lord, and he heard me; out of **the belly of hell** cried I, and thou heardest my voice.

³ **For thou hadst cast me into the deep, in the midst of the seas**; and the **floods compassed me about**: all thy billows and thy waves passed over me.

⁴ Then I said, I am cast out of thy sight; yet I will look again toward thy holy temple.

⁵ The waters compassed me about, even to the soul: the depth closed me round about, the weeds were wrapped about my head.

⁶ **I went down to the bottoms of the mountains; the earth with her bars was about me for ever: yet hast thou brought up my life from corruption, O Lord my God.**

⁷ When my soul fainted within me I remembered the Lord: and my prayer came in unto thee, into thine holy temple.

⁸ They that observe lying vanities forsake their own mercy.

⁹ But I will sacrifice unto thee with the voice of thanksgiving; I will pay that that I have vowed. Salvation is of the Lord.

¹⁰ And the Lord spake unto the fish, and it
vomited out Jonah upon the dry land.

Jonah obviously didn't go to hell. He is in the belly of
the whale. Even though he is in the belly of the whale—he
describes himself as being in the bottom of the mountains. He
says, "the earth with her bars was about me forever." This is
not literally about the whale's belly. We can say Jonah was
figuratively in hell—but not literally. We see this literally
being fulfilled with Jesus Christ:

Matthew 12:40

⁴⁰ For as Jonas was three days and three nights
in the whale's belly; so shall **the Son of man
be three days and three nights in the heart of
the earth.**

David also foreshadows the death, burial, and
resurrection of Jesus Christ:

Psalm 16:10

¹⁰ For thou wilt not leave my soul in hell;
neither wilt thou suffer thine Holy One to see
corruption.

David literally said this—but Jesus literally
experienced and fulfilled this:

Acts 2:27

²⁷ Because thou **wilt not leave my soul in hell**, neither wilt **thou suffer thine Holy One to see corruption.**

Again—we have *dual-prophecy fulfillments*—a *shadow fulfillment*—and then the more *dramatic fulfillment*. I will spend more time on how dual and triple-prophecy fulfillment applies specifically to the last days in the final section of this very important chapter.

TIMELINE OF THE LAST DAYS

There have been numerous debates over the Antichrist figure. This includes his identity and his timeline (rise to power and length of his ruling). Several have contended that the Antichrist has already come, and others argue that the Antichrist is not actually revealed in Daniel 9:27. They would argue the "he" in Daniel 9:27 is referring to the Messiah. I will deal with this specific argument thoroughly later in this chapter (after my extensive analysis of the 7-year timeline).

Remember—there are different camps in the world of eschatology. For example: there exists the futurist position and the historicist position. I am of course a futurist (pre-mill, post-trib, pre-wrath, futurist, to be exact). As I assume the reader has gathered by now—the futurist would say the majority of events in chapters such as Matthew 24, Mark 13, Luke 21, and books like Revelation, contain events that have not yet happened—and will happen in the future. Futurists ultimately look to the future for the fulfillment of many of the events found in these chapters and books. A futurist such as I would also say that Daniel's 70th week is still future and has not yet been fulfilled. A historicist on the other hand might say most of these prophecies have been fulfilled either literally or symbolically (or a mix) over the course of history. They may even say the Pope is the Antichrist. The futurist on the other hand would say there are many antichrists—but one major Antichrist in the future.

Preterists are those that believe most or all events in the book of Revelation, Matthew 24, Daniel, etc., have already occurred. They might point to the Antichrist as being Antiochus Epiphanes (Grecian leader), Nero or even Emperor Titus (who destroyed the temple and Jerusalem in 70 AD).

The problem preterists have is that although there have been numerous great shadows or types of Antichrists (Antiochus Epiphanes, Titus, Nero), there is still going to be one main Antichrist that essentially fulfills all the requirements provided in scripture for this one world leader. The Bible says there are many antichrists:

1 John 2:18

[18] Little children, it is the last time: and as ye have heard that **antichrist shall come**, even now are **there many antichrists**; whereby we know that it is the last time.

Notice we have many antichrists and one main Antichrist to come. Preterists—and even historicists to an extent—will take the many antichrists and yet ignore the one major Antichrist that shall come. Remember—when it comes to Bible prophecy—we have dual and triple prophecy fulfillments. This means we often have an immediate application and a future more dramatic fulfillment—the main event.

The Bible is clear in Revelation 13 (the pinnacle chapter dealing with the great tribulation and the reign of the Antichrist) that there will be a man who receives a deadly wound to his head. That deadly wound is healed, he steps into the temple, claims to be God, and the whole world worships after him. This is the man in Revelation 13 portrayed as ruling over a one world system—and an expression of that one world system is a one world currency and religion. The Bible tells us that all languages and nations will worship him (those not written in the book of life from the foundation of the world). It is absurd to reason that somebody like this has existed in the past. Yes—we have types of antichrists—but never have we seen anywhere in history a case where every single nation worshiped one man—and that one man ruled over the planet. Not only that—we have never seen any place in history where a "mark" (almost certainly a microchip of some form) was required, and whoever did not have this mark could not buy or sell—and as a consequence were killed. None of this has happened. The end times Antichrist will persist in power for 42 months (3.5 years) after the abomination of desolation (when he takes away the daily sacrifice and stands up as God).

This will be the start of the period known as the great tribulation.

Forty and two months:

Revelation 13:5-7

[5] **And there was given unto him a mouth speaking great things and blasphemies; and power was given unto him to continue forty and two months.**

[6] And he opened his mouth in blasphemy against God, to blaspheme his name, and his tabernacle, and them that dwell in heaven.

[7] And it was given unto him to make war with the saints, and to overcome them: and power was given him over all kindreds, and tongues, and nations.

We find a period of 1260 days—the first half of the 7-year period:

Revelation 12:6

6 And the woman fled into the wilderness, where she hath a place prepared of God, that they should feed her there a **thousand two hundred and threescore days.**

In Chapter 12 of Revelation, we are speaking about the first half of the 7 years. The Antichrist comes to power during this first half. The whole of humanity is effectively undergoing world war, famine, pestilence, inflation, and death. In Chapter 13 of Revelation, we see the abomination of desolation and the gaining of power by the Antichrist (midpoint/3.5 years). Do you see how all these numbers fit together perfectly as a 7-year period that basically starts with the Antichrist making an agreement with many, and then culminates with the millennial reign of Jesus Christ—where He comes back to this earth to set up His kingdom? To say any of this has happened has zero scriptural, logical, or historical support. Therefore, I say the preterist, postmillennial, and a-millennial (no Millennium) positions are careless and unsophisticated. They require the disregarding of a lot of data—including the clear structure of both Daniel and Revelation. These phony positions have no real compelling justification for why the numbers supplied (1260, 1290, 42 months, etc.) match up so perfectly within the book of Revelation chronologies, and with the 7-year period of Daniel's 70th week. Many who hold to these flawed and amateurish positions either spiritualize the numbers, assert they aren't of any real significance, or even (historicists) argue these numbers are in years (as mentioned earlier) and not days. No—the reason the Bible tells us repeatedly these numbers are in days—and even months (42 months) is because they are truly literal numbers and therefore a real period.

Remember—we have 3.5 years of tribulation (with the last 2-3 months of the tribulation being great tribulation) and the final 3.5 years being God's wrath.

To recap a bit—we have 7 years broken up into 2 halves. We know the Antichrist continues in power (when he attains full management and reverence) for 3.5 years (which is the second half). The second half commences at the abomination of desolation (which Paul says will come before the rapture). The week (week meaning a phase of 7 years—and not 7 days) begins when the Antichrist confirms a covenant with many. Since this agreement most likely occurs behind closed doors—we won't know when the week starts. From the abomination of desolation, we have 1290 days to the battle of Armageddon and the Millennium. Since the middle of the week is when the abomination of desolation takes place—we will know when we are practically 3.5 years into the week.

In addition to knowing when the abomination of desolation takes place—we also know *the rapture will take place 1335 days into Daniel's 70th week.* Now it is critical to understand that this is not a date setting—since we do not know when the week starts. But what we do know is that whenever this week starts (with the Antichrist confirming the covenant with many for 1 week), 1335 days into the start of this period will be the rapture—the day we as believers wait for (the day we get new bodies and are glorified).

Daniel 12:12

[12] Blessed is he that waiteth, and cometh to the **thousand three hundred and five and thirty days.**

Since the Bible informs us that from the abomination of desolation, we have 1290 days to the battle of Armageddon and the Millennium, we know the time between the Antichrist's full rise to power, and the sun and moon going dark (followed immediately by the rapture) is only a few months max. This brief period is the great tribulation—which is essentially a subset of the tribulation itself.

I also want the reader to notice in verse 10 of Revelation 16 that the Antichrist is still in power during God's wrath and the outpouring of the vial judgments:

Revelation 16:10

[10] And the fifth angel poured out his vial upon **the seat of the beast**; and **his kingdom** was full of darkness; and they gnawed their tongues for pain,

This verse is towards the **very end of the 7 years** when end times events are starting to wrap up. This is the pouring out of God's wrath (trumpets, vials). This is also shortly before the Millennium. We are at the 5th of the 7 vials in Revelation 16:10.

The word seat is like a government's seat. The seat of the beast is his capital or his headquarters. This is where the Antichrist dictates from. As my children might say: this is his lair. Kings rule from a throne and the Antichrist's power is the seat. While God's wrath is being poured out on the world of the wicked, the Antichrist still evidently has his place of world power. Therefore, it makes no sense to set the great tribulation as being 3.5 years—when the Antichrist is obviously ruling directly into the period of God's wrath. It is not precise to say the tribulation is 3.5 years and then the great tribulation is an additional 3.5 years. No—the roughly 75 days (1260-1335—which is the number of days to the rapture = -75) is the time of the great tribulation. This time is cut short according to the Bible:

Matthew 24:22

22 And except **those days should be shortened,** there should **no flesh be saved**: but for ***the elect's sake those days shall be shortened.***

If Christians had to withstand 3.5 years of intense persecution by the Antichrist and his one world army—no believer would be saved. This is why Jesus Christ tells us *those days will be shortened,* and *they will be shortened for the elect's sake.* Therefore, if we as believers endure to the end of the great tribulation—we will be saved physically—at the coming of the Lord.

Since the timeline of Daniel's 70th week is one of the most technical aspects of my model of eschatology—let me quickly reiterate a few points (I also encourage the reader to utilize the chart supplied at the end of this book that breaks all this information down carefully into visual form). The Antichrist is still ruling and reigning into the time of God's wrath. Since we know the Antichrist continues for 42 months/3.5 years, and this is the second half of Daniel's 70th week, then the Antichrist must rule into God's wrath (which is after the seals and the rapture). The abomination of desolation is at or near the midpoint of the week—which is 7 years. The second half is the reign of the Antichrist and God pours out His wrath during a portion of his reign.

The second half involves all of God's wrath, Antichrist ruling and reigning, the treading underfoot of Jerusalem by the gentiles (known as the times of the gentiles), and the preaching of the 2 witnesses (Moses and Elijah). Remember—Revelation 1-11 is a perfect chronological form, and then Revelation 12-22 is designed as another complete chronology. A supporting line of evidence is the use of "after these things". This tells us the trumpets and the vials come after the seals, after the sun and moon are darkened, and after the rapture.

The 7-year period is essentially broken down into:

1260 years of tribulation – 75 days of Great Tribulation – 1215 days of Wrath,

1260 – 1335 = -75 days.

Daniel 12:11

[11] And from the time that the daily sacrifice shall be taken away, and the abomination that maketh desolate set up, there shall be **a thousand two hundred and ninety days.**

I am sure the reader has noticed Daniel 12:11 isn't exactly 1260 days—it is in fact 1290 days. Why is this? Well, the answer is fairly simple. The discrepancy is due to the

Bible's calendar of 30-day months. Every month is 30 days. This is distinct from our days today since we only have 30-day months with September, April, June, and November. All the rest have 31 days with February having 28. We do not have a clean year of 360 days broken up into 12 periods of 30 days.

Since the Bible's calendar is different from ours (we have 365 days rather than 360), a system such as the Bible's necessitates the addition of *1 extra month every 6 years.* This keeps everything in line with the seasons. This is a required adjustment since without it we would ultimately be having summer in December and winter in July. Adding 1 extra month every 6 years sidesteps this problem. We have to make sure we are staying in line with the sun and the rotation of the earth. It is also helpful that we have 1290 days to make it easier to determine which number is the 1st half (1260) of the week and which is the 2nd (1290).

Daniel's 70th week is a period of 7 years. Therefore—we are going to need to account for a leap month. And this is exactly why the first half of the 7 years is 1260 and the second half is 1290. Pretty simple right? This amounts to 1260 plus a bonus of 30 days. And this would round out to a full 7 years. 1260 days is precisely 42 months of 30 days and 1290 is correctly 43 months of 30 days. From the time the daily sacrifice shall be taken away (the midpoint), there shall be 1290 days (the second half). By understanding this, we are given more reason to believe that 1290 is the second part of the week since it would not be until year 6 that 30 days need to be added. And again—the Bible tells us that we are blessed if we wait and come to the 1335 days—which is the rapture. 1335 days into the first half of Daniel's 70th week—which is

1260 days—leaves us with 75 days for great tribulation. At first this may seem perplexing—but after you study it out carefully—you will be absolutely fascinated at how amazingly all this fits—which is a fit the false eschatological positions are powerless to account for!

In a nutshell:

-    1260 days into the week is the abomination of desolation,

-    1335 days in is the rapture (since it's the day believers wait for—the redemption of our bodies),

-    This leaves us with basically 75 days—but to be safe one could say "up to 3 months of great tribulation",

-    The Antichrist gets full power and control (where he is worshiped as God on earth) at the midpoint, but he only gets to enjoy it for a few months—because the rest of his 42-month rule is spent dealing with the pouring out of God's wrath,

-    1260 days = first half,

-    1290 days = second half,

-    1260 and a bonus 30 (leap month)

- 1335 days from the beginning of the week to the Rapture (53% mark)

- 75 days of great tribulation.

THE "HE" OF DANIEL 9:27

There has been considerable debate on the identity of the "he" in verse 27 of Daniel 9. Even though the passage is clearly referring to the future Antichrist (which I will thoroughly demonstrate), many (mainly preterists) have claimed that verse 27 is actually the Messiah—Jesus Christ.

Daniel 9:27

[27] And he shall confirm the covenant with many for one week: and in the midst of the week he shall cause the sacrifice and the oblation to cease, and for the overspreading of abominations he shall make it desolate, even until the consummation, and that determined shall be poured upon the desolate.

Firstly—this is the final week—the 70th week. In verses 24-27 of Daniel 9—we've seen 3 components to the 70 weeks of prophecy. We have the 7 weeks, the 62 weeks (69 weeks with a gap), and then a final week (which we are discussing now). I have demonstrated earlier in this chapter how we have 2 gaps in these 70 weeks—1 gap between the 7th and 8th weeks and then another gap between the 69th and 70th week (with the 70th week primarily being future).

It is important to note that it was at the end of the 69th week that Jesus Christ died and rose again. The 70th week hadn't even started yet. Therefore—the Ministry of Jesus Christ—the Messiah—cannot be put into the first half of Daniel's 70th week (as some partial preterists have attempted to argue). The first fulfillment of Daniel's 70 weeks is the 7 weeks, then the 62 weeks, and it is after the second component of the 70 weeks that Messiah is cut off (69 weeks). I have proven that Messiah being cut off is a clear reference to Jesus Christ dying for the world:

Daniel 9:25-26

25 Know therefore and understand, that from the going forth of the commandment to restore and to build Jerusalem unto the Messiah the Prince shall be **seven weeks**, and **threescore and two weeks**: the street shall be built again, and the wall, even in **troublous times.**

26 And after **threescore and two weeks** shall Messiah be cut off, but not for himself: and the **people of the prince that shall come shall destroy the city and the sanctuary**; and the end thereof shall be with a flood, and unto the end of the war desolations are determined.

Based on the entirety of verse 26 of Daniel 9, we know that after Jesus dies on the cross, somebody is going to come and destroy the temple. Jesus also predicted the destruction of Jerusalem and the temple in Matthew 24:

Matthew 24:2-4

[2] And Jesus said unto them, See ye not all these things? verily I say unto you, **There shall not be left here one stone upon another, that shall not be thrown down.**

[3] And as he sat upon the mount of Olives, the disciples came unto him privately, saying, Tell us, when shall these things be? and what shall be the sign of thy coming, and of the end of the world?

[4] And Jesus answered and said unto them, Take heed that no man deceive you.

In 70 AD this amazing prophecy was fulfilled with **Commander Titus** (a foreshadowing of the future Antichrist) and **his Roman Army**. His Army destroyed the temple for a second time. Remarkably—this Jewish-Roman war lasted 7 years (from 66 AD to 73 AD) and in the middle of the war, Titus and his army destroyed the temple (70 AD). This was roughly 3.5 years into the war—in the middle of the "week". Titus essentially desolates the temple mid week/mid war.

The Jewish-Roman war started in 66 AD and ended in 73 AD. This war lasted 7 years, and the sacrifices ceased right in the middle of the war (roughly 3.5 years in).

Daniel 9 predicts the rebuilding of Jerusalem and the temple. It also predicts the Messiah being killed (and not for Himself). And we also have another astonishingly specific prediction that ends up being partially (since dual and triple prophecy applies here) fulfilled from 66 to 73 AD. Remember—the Jewish-Roman war started in 66 AD and ended in 73 AD. This war lasted 7 years, and the sacrifices discontinued right in the middle of the war (roughly 3.5 years in). This prediction was the burning and destruction of Jerusalem and the temple. We also have the 7-year war predicted. Verses 24-27 contain predictions that prove the Bible truly is the Word of God. These are confirmed predictions that have perplexed skeptics for centuries. Critics of the Bible have offered nothing persuasive in response to this incredible evidence for the inspiration of the Bible from prophecy.

Remember—prophecies in the Bible have dual fulfillment, and triple fulfillment where we normally have a shadow fulfillment and then a more literal exact fulfillment in the end. This is typically where preterists go wrong when interpreting Bible prophecy. They think because a lot of this was partially—or even fully fulfilled in the spiritual sense (Jesus' conquering during His first coming spiritually), then it is complete—with nothing left in the future. They forget that the reason many of these prophecies lack the fulfillment of all their specific details is essentially because they still have a much more dramatic fulfillment awaiting in the future. We have shadow fulfillments and then the main event, and the main event is described comprehensively in Revelation.

The 7-year period that comprises the discontinuing of the daily sacrifice, the destruction of the temple at the hands of a prince and his people is all perfectly consistent with known history. We discussed the 7-year Jewish-Roman war where, right in the middle of the war (the approximately 3.5-year mark), the temple was destroyed—and as a result—the sacrifice was stopped. The war is also 7 years (as predicted). It starts in 66 AD and ends in 73 AD. Again—this is a wonderful, fulfilled prophecy. Bible interpreters get into trouble when they take this impressive, confirmed prediction and then argue that this was it—and there is nothing future. It is of utmost importance that we acknowledge the reality of a foreshadowing to a main event in Bible prophecy. For example: we have both Antiochus Epiphanes and Titus acting as foreshadows to the main Antichrist in the end times.

Comparing the book of Daniel to the book of Revelation makes things extremely clear. We have a 7-year period and in the midst of this 7-year period, the Antichrist comes to full power. He receives a deadly wound which is healed. The world is then deceived by him. They look to him as the second coming—or the Messiah. We know there is also a false prophet that will help convince the world that the Antichrist is the real deal—which results in the worship of him. We also know that an image is made that can speak. This image will be set up, and all those who do not worship the image will be killed. None of this has happened yet. Yes—we had a 7-year war from 66 to 73 AD where in the middle of this war—the temple was destroyed. I am not contesting this. What we have in this instance is an amazing foreshadowing of the main event—which we read about in Revelation.

Much of what is written in Daniel has an immediate application to the people of that day—but also a future application in the end times. For example, when we read about the little horn in Daniel 7—we see a clear foreshadowing of Titus—the Roman leader (who eventually becomes the Roman emperor). We do have an application for this in 70 AD—since his army (the people of the prince) destroyed the temple. Then in chapter 8 of Daniel—we see another foreshadowing of the future end times Antichrist with Antiochus Epiphanes. In chapter 7 we read about the little horn of the fourth kingdom (Rome and the end times one world system), but in chapter 8 we are given a detailed description of the little horn that comes out of the third kingdom—which is Greece. We see Antiochus Epiphanes in chapter 11 as well.

The preterists will respond by asking "if these events have already happened—why are you saying it will happen again—on a grandeur scale?" Remember—the preterist mentality is essentially "if it's done, it's done." Unfortunately—these types of questions and responses from the preterists again demonstrate their lack of ability to understand dual and triple Bible prophecy fulfillment. Antiochus Epiphanes (a type of antichrist even before the coming of Jesus Christ), and Titus did not fulfill the prophecies of Daniel in their fullness. This is why preterists have to basically accuse the Bible of some serious exaggerations—when in fact the Bible is not exaggerating at all—there is truly a main event in the future. These prophecies need to be fully fulfilled. There are many details that have not yet occurred, and will occur in the future. The foreshadowing events have only manifested partial fulfillments of these significant Bible prophecies.

The first coming of Christ, and the destruction of the temple in 70 AD both fulfilled many of these prophecies symbolically and partially—but not entirely. For example: in the 2nd century BC, Antiochus Epiphanes declared himself to be God. There have been coins discovered that represent this 2nd century Grecian leader as God manifest. But I want the reader to ask themselves "did the entire world worship this man?" Of course not. All nations, tongues, and kindreds, did not worship Antiochus Epiphanes—nor did Titus receive worldwide worship. This is the whole point of a foreshadowing to a main event. We get minor details—with the major details saved for the future. Did these antichrist types require a mark of all people? And that those who would not receive this mark would be prevented from buying or selling, and would be killed? Again—the answer is no. This is because not all the specifics of these prophecies have occurred. But they will occur in the future. There will one day be a mark made mandatory that whoever does not receive this mark will be killed, or will suffer since they can no longer buy or sell.

I challenge the preterists to show me any documentation from the Grecian and Roman empires of the universal instituting of a mark that was mandatory for all people, and those that refused it were killed. These details cannot be provided by the preterist—which is why they are forced to spiritualize most of the details contained in these prophecies. If preterism is true—the Bible has really been exaggerating the details of these important events. Everything that has occurred with Antiochus Epiphanes and the 7-year Jewish-Roman war was extremely minor compared to what awaits us in the future. If you don't believe me—just read the book of Revelation.

Everything that occurred with the Grecian empire, Antiochus Epiphanes, and the destruction of the temple in 70 AD is a great picture of what is going to occur in the future with the one world government, the Antichrist, the false prophet, and the mark of the beast. Don't let the preterist deceive you. The Bible is not overly exaggerating the details of these events. These events described in Daniel and Revelation are not minor events—they are worldwide in scale. Yes—the immediate fulfillments and applications were minor—but the literal dramatic fulfillment will be major:

Revelation 13:7-8

[7] And it was given unto him to make war with the **saints**, and to **overcome them**: and **power was given him over all kindreds, and tongues, and nations.**

[8] **And all that dwell upon the earth shall worship him**, whose names are not written in the book of life of the Lamb slain from the foundation of the world.

Notice when the Bible describes the main event in Revelation—we have a scope that is worldwide in scale—rather than local. The entire earth is said to worship the Antichrist and his one world regime. Matthew 24 tells us that this world will experience tribulation and trouble that has never been seen before:

Matthew 24:15-22

[15] When ye therefore shall see the abomination of desolation, spoken of by Daniel the prophet, stand in the holy place, (whoso readeth, let him understand:)

[16] Then let them which be in Judaea flee into the mountains:

[17] Let him which is on the housetop not come down to take any thing out of his house:

[18] Neither let him which is in the field return back to take his clothes.

[19] And woe unto them that are with child, and to them that give suck in those days!

[20] But pray ye that your flight be not in the winter, neither on the sabbath day:

[21] **For then shall be great tribulation, such as was not since the beginning of the world to this time, no, nor ever shall be.**

[22] **And except those days should be shortened, there should no flesh be saved: but for the elect's sake those days shall be shortened.**

These eye-opening verses would make no sense if preterism was true. It is impossible to argue that the events associated with Antiochus Epiphanes and the 7-year Jewish-Roman war were the worst events to ever occur on this planet. Yes, the details of these events are devastating—but they were local events. These events were significant to the part of the world they occurred in—but in terms of full scope—they were not the types of events described in Matthew 24 and Revelation.

Preterists, amillennialists, and postmillennialists reduce the prophecies found in Daniel, Matthew 24, and Revelation to basically nothing. The happenings of Revelation are not minor like those that hold to these various false eschatological positions want to claim. The cataclysms described in Revelation through the trumpet and vial judgments are devastating. To say these cataclysms have already occurred, or are simply symbolic, is to not believe what the text is saying. Essentially—it is only the premillennialists that believe these events will actually take place in their completeness. Sorry preterists—but God is not just "scaring" us with all these extraordinary catastrophes that apparently aren't going to happen. The events of Revelation will happen, and these preterists are reducing their significance.

***

There is an extremely wrong interpretation made by partial preterists. This erroneous interpretation says verse 27 of Daniel 9 is actually about Jesus, and not the Antichrist. Jesus is the one acting in verse 27 according to these preterist apologists. Firstly—the easiest way to prove verse 27 is the Antichrist is to show that the last singular noun mentioned is "prince"—as in "people of the prince that shall come". *This "prince" is the antecedent to the pronoun "he".* As I have covered thoroughly—the prince that shall come in "the people of the prince that shall come" is Titus—the Roman General. And the people of this prince (Titus) are the Roman army. The prince is clearly not Jesus in this verse. The people of Jesus are believers—the elect—not the Roman army. One could argue that God used the Roman army as an instrument to carry out His punishment, but that is not equivalent to being His people. No—His people are believers—the saints.

We know (based on scripture and history) it is Titus and his army that destroyed the temple. This destruction occurred in 70 AD. Again—history confirms this. This epic foreshadowing to the age of the Antichrist in the last days is basically removed in order to adopt this absurd preterist based argument.

The "he" in verse 27 is therefore logically referring to the "prince that shall come". Again—what is the most recent noun this could be an antecedent of (I urge the reader to reread Daniel 9:24-27)? The pronoun has an antecedent, and so when we see a "he", we understand it is referring to a person. That person we just read about is the *prince that shall come.* This was literally referring to Titus—the Roman prince, whose army destroyed the temple and the city in 70 AD. A lot of twisting and stretching is required to deny this. It is clear—Jesus Christ is not the one carrying out the abomination of desolation.

Chapter 9 of Daniel is factually describing aspects of the 7-year Jewish-Roman war that saw Titus and his army destroy the temple. But this is all a shadow of what's to come—a shadow of the more dramatic worldwide fulfillment in the end times with the actual Antichrist—the final boss.

In addition to everything being said, I want to point out an interesting observation in Daniel. The 70 years of Babylonian captivity culminates with Israel returning to the promised land. These 70 years basically conclude with a happy ending. The 70 weeks (not to be confused with the 70 years) ultimately culminates with believers in the promised land for the millennial reign of Jesus Christ. The 70 weeks ends with a resurrection of the dead. This resurrection is composed of all saints (believers) of all time who will rule and reign with Jesus Christ for 1000 years (when all spiritual Israel shall be saved). If the reader is following everything being said so far in this chapter—you will probably recognize this beautiful shadow fulfillment—with the 70-year captivity being the shadow fulfillment, and the 70 weeks being the literal more dramatic fulfillment. *The 70 weeks ends with a literal kingdom.*

I urge those that hold to a futurist, premill view of eschatology to avoid preterist traps. The easiest way to demolish the preterist position is to acknowledge the reality of Daniel's 70th week in 1st century AD with the 7-year Jewish-Roman war and Titus and his army destroying the temple. 70 AD represented the middle of the week when the temple was destroyed and 73 AD represented the end of this 7 year period (a war in this case). But where the preterist goes wrong is not recognizing the fact that this was not a complete fulfillment. The 1st century realization of Daniel's 70th week was a shadow of what the book of Revelation describes as the last days with a real Antichrist and a real one world system. This will be a time of tribulation that the world has never seen.

Another example of a dual and triple prophecy is the abomination of desolation. We had an abomination of desolation in the 2nd century BC, and we had one in the 1st century AD. But in the end times, we will have the third and most dramatic abomination of desolation (the one described by Jesus in Matthew 24). Antiochus Epiphanes (described in Daniel 8 and 11), was a Greek prince in 2nd century BC who came in and corrupted the Jewish temple. He set up a statue of Zeus at the temple in Jerusalem. This was the abomination of desolation. He essentially stood up an abomination—a pagan idol in the house of God. This was of course an abomination and a desecration. History seems to tell us he offered up a sacrifice—which was a pig. As we can see, the taking away of the sacrifice and the abomination of desolation are a package deal. They happen at the same time, by the same person. This is another reason why it makes no sense to claim the "he" of Daniel 9:27 is the Messiah. This is to say that Jesus Christ is the one who sets up the abomination of desolation. This is simply not true.

Full and partial preterists have a very weak case here in Daniel 9:27. As we have seen, the most logical reading of the text tells us that the "he" is both Titus *and* the end times Antichrist. This is because the last singular noun mentioned is prince (people of the prince that shall come). This prince is the immediate antecedent.

Some preterists will desperately argue that the antecedent can't be the prince of the people since the verse mentions the "people" rather than just the "prince". This is an absurd argument, and there is no law in grammar that convincingly implies this argument is valid. Just because it is an object of a preposition does not stop it from being the antecedent. These rescue devices are not compelling.

What if I said: "I went over to my friend's house, and he gave me coffee"? This is a perfectly rational way to indicate my friend served me coffee. If I said, "I went to the house of my friend, and we had coffee together", I am implying that it is the friend and I having coffee. The object of a preposition can still be the antecedent of a subject pronoun. This is basic grammar.

ANTICHRIST TAKES AWAY THE SACRIFICE

By now—the reader should understand clearly why dual and triple prophecy fulfillment is so critical when studying last-days theology. Since Titus was just a foreshadowing of the Antichrist—it is not required that he fulfill every detail of Daniel 9:26-27. What occurred in 70 AD was a fulfillment yes, but only a shadow fulfillment. The city and temple were destroyed. Since the temple was destroyed, the sacrifice was stopped. These known historical details correlate amazingly with the prophecy of Daniel 9. But the far more dramatic fulfillment will occur during Daniel's 70th week (the 7-year period in the end times). Futurists can essentially say both are true. Titus and the destruction of Jerusalem is true, and a future Daniel's 70th week (comprising the Antichrist and his reign) is also true.

Verse 27 of Daniel 9 tells us that the Antichrist will confirm a covenant with many for one week. Titus and his Roman army destroyed the temple, and the Jewish-Roman war lasted 7 years. But did Titus confirm a covenant with many? Not necessarily. He doesn't have to—since this is only one application of the prophecy of Daniel's 70 weeks. We know the Antichrist will confirm a covenant, or make an agreement with many in the end times. This will be a necessary step in his rise to full power and control. If the Antichrist—and the dragon—want full control over the earth, there will be agreements that have to be made. It would be very difficult to come to power (the type of power that grants you absolute authority over the entire earth) without making an agreement or covenant. A person does not come to power unilaterally. It's simply not that easy. The Antichrist has alliances he needs to make. He does not rise to power in an instant—it is a rise to power that occurs over time. He goes out to conquer when the first seal is open at the start of the tribulation period, but is not fully revealed to the world as the Antichrist until the abomination of desolation—which is roughly 3.5 years into the 7 years. The initial deal he makes at the start of the week may just take place behind closed doors. This means a lot of his rise to power is occurring without us knowing much about it. A shift this big in geopolitics will require time and effort. Logically it makes sense that the Antichrist would make a covenant. Yes—God makes covenants—but this does not necessitate interpreting verse 27 as being about Jesus. All kinds of people make covenants and deals. People make agreements every single day. Just because a "covenant" is being talked about in Daniel 9 does not automatically mean this is a "good" covenant, or an agreement made by God.

PRETERISTS CHALLENGE FUTURISTS

What is a covenant? A covenant is essentially a deal, or an agreement made with somebody. Preterists repeatedly challenge futurists to show them one place in the entire Bible where the Antichrist is making a covenant. They advance this challenge thinking futurists can't answer it. This is another really bizarre line of argumentation employed by preterists. For a preterist to challenge a futurist to show them where the Antichrist makes an agreement in scripture (a challenge posed as a "gotcha" argument) tells me they are either just repeating an argument they have heard from one of their favorite preterist apologists—or have simply not read the relevant passages on this issue. Verses 21-24 of Daniel 11 answers this preterist challenge, and answers it quite easily:

Daniel 11:21-24

²¹ And in his estate shall stand up a vile person, to whom they shall not give the honour of the kingdom: but he shall come in peaceably, and obtain the kingdom by flatteries.

²² And with the arms of a flood shall they be overflown from before him, and shall be broken; yea, also the prince of the covenant.

²³ **And after the league made with him he shall work deceitfully**: for he shall come up, and shall become strong with a small people.

²⁴ **He shall enter peaceably even upon the fattest places of the province;** and he shall do that which his fathers have not done, nor his fathers' fathers; he shall scatter among them the prey, and spoil, and riches: yea, and he shall forecast his devices against the strong holds, even for a time.

Notice: "**And after the league made with him he shall work deceitfully**". What we have here is the Antichrist making a league with people. He makes this league with many, but then works deceitfully by not following through with this agreement made. He is ultimately making a league or a covenant with many simply to get full power and authority over the earth. His final goal is to have all world leaders hand their power and authority to him. In accomplishing this—the Antichrist will be the one world ruler. Basically, he makes a league with a group of people, and then eventually breaks it when he's accomplished what he needs, or does what the Antichrist is prophesied to do. This line of argumentation employed by preterists is formulated based on a severe lack of sophistication. What I mean by that is preterists are challenging futurists to show them where the Antichrist is making a covenant with people, but they are advancing this challenge not understanding that different words are used in the Bible to describe the same thing. We see this also with the abomination of desolation. It is also described as the transgression of desolation. Therefore, preterists who are only looking for the word abomination when examining this future event are at risk of missing out on important information. This information would be pertaining to this major end times event. There are different words used to describe the same event (league/covenant, transgression/abomination).

What is a league exactly? A league is a type of treaty where people join together (for example: the League of Nations). The Antichrist forms a league and then deals deceitfully. This is him confirming the covenant with many for one week (7 years). In the middle of this 7-year period—the Antichrist essentially goes back on what he agreed he would do.

Daniel 11 is a very deep and complicated chapter that comprises a dual prophecy. These verses in Daniel 11 have an application in 2nd century BC with Antiochus Epiphanes—but it also has an end times application that points to the Antichrist and his rise to power. Remember—there was an abomination of desolation with Antiochus Epiphanes, a type of abomination of desolation with Titus (since he destroyed the temple), but also a future more dramatic abomination of desolation (that Jesus and the book of Revelation talk about) in the end times with the Antichrist and the rebuilt third temple. Daniel 11 is a more than sufficient answer to this commonly repeated preterist challenge.

Preterists have no compelling response to why the days provided in scripture (1260, 1290, 42 months, 3.5 years) correlate so perfectly with Daniel's 70th week being future and comprising 7 years. They want to say the "he" in Daniel 9:27 is not the Antichrist—and yet the book of Revelation makes it clear there's going to be an Antichrist and he continues in power (at the abomination of desolation where the daily sacrifice is cut off) for 42 months! This is at the midpoint of the week. *Daniel 9:27 tells us **clearly** that whoever this "he" is will stop the daily sacrifice approximately 3.5 years into the week!* This fits so perfectly with what we know about the Antichrist that it is absolutely absurd to argue this isn't the Antichrist—even though Daniel 7, 8, 11, and 12 all corroborate Daniel 9:27 as being him. The book of Revelation is clear—the Antichrist will continue in power for 3.5 years (42 months). We also see the numbers 1260 and 1290 used (as I covered extensively in the timeline portion of this book). The debate is over—Daniel's 70th week is still in the future.

Daniel 11 and 12 both demonstrate it is indeed the Antichrist that causes the sacrifice to cease:

Daniel 11:31

³¹ And arms shall stand on his part, and they shall pollute the sanctuary of strength, and **shall take away the daily sacrifice**, and **they shall place the abomination that maketh desolate.**

Daniel 12:11

**<u>¹¹ And from the time that the daily sacrifice
shall be taken away, and the abomination
that maketh desolate set up, there shall be a
thousand two hundred and ninety days.</u>**

The fact that the nearest antecedent in these hotly
debated verses is the prince—the people of the
prince—should be enough evidence to end this debate. The
antecedent clearly indicates it is both Titus (in terms of the
shadow fulfillment) and the end times Antichrist being
referred to. The "he" is referring to the prince of the people,
and not to the Messiah before it. Even though this reality is
enough to demonstrate the "he" is the Antichrist—we still
have an abundance of additional evidence supporting this
conclusion.

Daniel chapter 8 describes the little horn, which is a
picture of the Antichrist. And when talking about the little
horn in verse 11 of Daniel 8, the Bible portrays the little horn
as being the one who takes away the daily sacrifice:

Daniel 8:9-11

⁹ And out of one of them came forth a **little
horn**, which waxed exceeding great, toward
the south, and toward the east, and toward the
pleasant land.

¹⁰ And it waxed great, even to the host of
heaven; and it cast down some of the host and

of the stars to the ground, and stamped upon them.

11 Yea, he magnified himself even to the prince of the host, and by him the daily sacrifice was taken away, and the place of the sanctuary was cast down.

In verses 12 and 13 of Daniel 8 we read it is the Antichrist who is against the daily sacrifice:

Daniel 8:12-13

12 And an host was given him against the daily sacrifice by reason of transgression, and it cast down the truth to the ground; and it practised, and prospered.

13 Then I heard one saint speaking, and another saint said unto that certain saint which spake, **How long shall be the vision concerning the daily sacrifice, and the transgression of desolation, to give both the sanctuary and the host to be trodden under foot?**

There is no doubt that in chapter 8 of Daniel—it is the little horn—the Antichrist—who is taking away the daily sacrifice. Therefore, why should we believe the "he" in Daniel 9:27 that is taking away the daily sacrifice is somebody different? Especially when these verses all correlate so beautifully. The Antichrist is the one who sets up the transgression of desolation—not Jesus.

As I pointed to earlier—Daniel 11 also clearly tells us it is the Antichrist taking away the daily sacrifice and setting up the abomination of desolation:

Daniel 11:31

[31] And arms shall stand on his part, and they shall pollute the sanctuary of strength, and **shall take away the daily sacrifice**, and **they shall place the abomination that maketh desolate.**

By whom is the sacrifice taken away? By the little horn—the Antichrist. And who sets up the abomination of desolation? Again—it is the Antichrist! *The same person who is taking away the daily sacrifice is also setting up the abomination of desolation.*

We have Daniel chapters 7, 8, 11, and 12 all representing the Antichrist, and yet we are to believe that Daniel chapter 9 is different? With no real compelling justification? These preterists are really grasping at straws. To argue Daniel's 70th week has all been fulfilled, and there is no future final week has no Biblical support. It is in fact an indefensible position. Preterists argue for Jesus as being the "he" in Daniel 9:27, and as a result making Jesus as the one who sets up the abomination of desolation—since the same person who takes away the daily sacrifice is also the person who sets up the transgression of desolation. Sorry preterists—but Jesus is not installing an abomination. Again—to argue that the subject of Daniel 9:27 is Jesus the Messiah is based on only reading chapter 9 and ignoring chapters 7, 8, 11, and 12. When we allow the Bible to define and explain itself—we can only come to one logical conclusion. That conclusion is that the "he" of Daniel 9:27 is the Antichrist. It fits like a glove. It is sloppy Biblical hermeneutics to isolate one chapter and ignore the others.

THE LITTLE HORN OF DANIEL 8

This last segment of the chapter will encompass many significant points. These points will assist the reader in better understanding dual-prophecy fulfillment. Remember—the world works in cycles—and so do prophecies. There is nothing new under the sun. Futurists get into trouble when debating preterists when they refuse to admit that much of what we read about in Daniel has already happened. We as futurists should not hesitate to admit this. Many of the events found in the book of Daniel have already occurred. But remember—they've only occurred on a minor scale, and not every single detail of these events has come to pass. This means that although several of these events have taken place—they will also happen again. And when they occur again—they will be far more dramatic than what we understand transpired in history (with Antiochus Epiphanes in the 2nd century BC, and Titus in 70 AD).

For better understanding—I want to spend some time here recapping several things I discussed earlier in this chapter. The reader will remember that in the 2nd chapter of Daniel—we learn about the great image that King Nebuchadnezzar dreamed about. The image included a head of gold, the shoulders and arms of silver, the loins of brass, the legs of iron, and the feet that were mingled with iron and clay. This image comprises 4 main sections—or 5 elements when we consider the toes that are mingled with the iron and clay. The components of this great image signify 4 great Kingdoms. King Nebuchadnezzar represented the head of gold. He was the King of Babylon. Then we have the representations of Medo-Persia, Greece, and then the Roman empire.

In Daniel 7 we learn about an analogous vision—except in this vision the kingdoms are being exemplified by 4 great beasts—or animals. These beasts in Daniel 7 are the lion (King Nebuchadnezzar and the Babylonians), a bear (the Medo-Persians), a leopard (Alexander the Great and the Grecian empire), and then the fourth beast being dreadful exceedingly with iron teeth (Rome and the future one world government). The fourth beast is portrayed as having 10 horns. The 10 horns signify 10 kings. The Bible tells us that after the 10 kings—another little horn surfaced. And this little horn had a mouth speaking great things—which correlates perfectly with the Antichrist in Revelation 13. This little horn is described as making war with the saints and prevailing against them. We see this resemblance in Revelation 13 with the Antichrist (ruler of the one world system) also making war with the saints and overcoming them. What we see between Daniel 7 and Revelation 13 are indisputable parallels linking the little horn of Daniel 7 with the Antichrist in Revelation. This little horn comes after the 10 kings of the fourth kingdom (Titus in 70 AD but the Antichrist in the last days).

Daniel 8:20-27

[20] **The ram** which thou sawest having **two horns** are the **kings of Media and Persia.**

[21] And **the rough goat** is the **king of Grecia**: and **the great horn** that is between his eyes is the **first king.**

[22] Now that being broken, whereas four stood up for it, four kingdoms shall stand up out of the nation, but not in his power.

[23] And in the latter time of their kingdom, when the transgressors are come to the full, a king of fierce countenance, and understanding dark sentences, shall stand up.

[24] And his power shall be mighty, but not by his own power: and he shall destroy wonderfully, and shall prosper, and practise, and shall destroy the mighty and the holy people.

[25] And through his policy also he shall cause craft to prosper in his hand; and he shall magnify himself in his heart, and by peace shall destroy many: he shall also stand up against the Prince of princes; but he shall be broken without hand.

26 And the vision of the evening and the morning which was told is true: wherefore shut thou up the vision; for it shall be for many days.

27 And I Daniel fainted, and was sick certain days; afterward I rose up, and did the king's business; and I was astonished at the vision, but none understood it.

In verse 3 of Daniel 8—we read about the same ram we just saw in verse 20. This ram had two horns—which correspond to the kings of Media and Persia. Verse 3 also describes the ram as having one horn that was higher than the other, and the higher one came up last:

Daniel 8:3

3 Then I lifted up mine eyes, and saw, and, behold, there stood before the river **a ram** which had **two horns**: and the **two horns were high**; but **one was higher than the other, and the higher came up last.**

The reason why one horn is higher than the other is because the king of Persia was greater than the king of the Medes. The latter of these two was more formidable and was higher than the other.

In verse 4 of Daniel 8, we are given a picture of the Medo-Persian army pushing in different directions and conquering—it cannot be beaten—or overcome. This is an empire that at the time cannot be overthrown.

It is in verse 5 that we read about the goat (which represents the Grecian empire). We understand from chapter 7 of Daniel, and history itself, that the Grecian empire came after the Medo-Persian empire (and the Medo-Persian empire came after the Babylonian rule). In chapter 7, the Grecian empire is represented as a leopard. This makes sense since we know that Alexander the Great (the notable horn on the goat) and Greece were renowned for their extraordinary speed. He is a well-known king who was able to move into different territories quickly and win battles. The mobility and speed of the Greeks (under the rule of Alexander the Great) were 2 of their most impressive assets. Daniel chapter 8 represents the Grecian empire (and Alexander the Great) as a goat that doesn't touch the ground as it runs—which again entails great speed:

Daniel 8:5-8

[5] And as I was considering, behold, an he goat came from the west on the face of the whole earth, and **touched not the ground**: and the goat had a notable horn between his eyes.

[6] And he came to the ram that had two horns, which I had seen standing before the river, and ran unto him in the fury of his power.

[7] And I saw him come close unto the ram, and he was moved with choler against him, and smote the ram, and brake his two horns: and there was no power in the ram to stand before him, but he cast him down to the ground, and

stamped upon him: and there was none that could deliver the ram out of his hand.

8 Therefore the he goat waxed very great: and when he was strong, the great horn was broken; and for it came up four notable ones toward the four winds of heaven.

The notable horn in verse 5 is referring to Alexander the Great, and the great horn that was broken in verse 8 is still referring to him. What this verse is informing us is that Alexander the Great experienced a sudden and unexpected death (remember—these are all incredibly accurate prophecies—that were fulfilled). We understand this from historical records. Alexander the Great died at a young age. Evidently, he got drunk, suffered a fever the next morning, lost his speech, and died a few weeks later. Since he died at such a young age—and unpredictably—there was not an obvious replacement (somebody to take his place). Disagreements resulted from a lack of clarity in terms of a successor, and what followed was a division in the kingdom. The kingdom was divided amongst his four great generals—which resulted in 4 separate kingdoms. This is why Daniel 7 represents the Grecian empire as having 4 wings and 4 heads:

Daniel 7:6

6 After this I beheld, and lo another**, like a leopard**, which had upon the back of it **four wings of a fowl**; the beast had also **four heads**; and dominion was given to it.

I want to take a quick moment to again point out the precision of these prophecies. It is fascinating to think about just how detailed they are. *Daniel was literally shown the future of the world.* He was given visions of kingdoms that had not yet appeared on the earth. And these visions were incredibly detailed and specific—as we can see in this chapter. The book of Daniel is irrefutable evidence for the inspiration of the Bible. The Bible is God's Word. And we need to believe it.

Verse 8 also makes the point about how the kingdom is divided into 4. It describes four notable ones coming up and taking over. At this point in the Grecian empire—the kingdom comprised multiple regions. These are the four kingdoms that continued the Grecian empire—but instead of one major kingdom—it was essentially four separate kingdoms that lacked a central power with a main ruler.

This is where I want to get to the focus of this section of the chapter:

Daniel 8:9-14

⁹ **And out of one of them came forth a little horn,** which waxed exceeding great, toward the south, and toward the east, and toward the pleasant land.

¹⁰ And it waxed great, even to the host of heaven; and it cast down some of the host and of the stars to the ground, and stamped upon them.

¹¹ Yea, **he magnified himself even to the prince of the host**, and **by him the daily sacrifice was taken away, and the place of the sanctuary was cast down.**

¹² And an host was given him against the daily sacrifice by reason of transgression, and it cast down the truth to the ground; and it practised, and prospered.

¹³ Then I heard one saint speaking, and another saint said unto that certain saint which spake, **How long shall be the vision concerning the daily sacrifice, and the transgression of desolation, to give both the sanctuary and the host to be trodden under foot?**

¹⁴ And he said unto me, Unto two thousand and three hundred days; then shall the sanctuary be cleansed.

Here is where we see another little horn—but this little horn is not the same as in Daniel chapter 7 (which was the Antichrist of Revelation 13). The little horn of Daniel 7 came up out of the fourth kingdom (the Roman empire and the one world system). The little horn in Daniel chapter 8 comes out of the Grecian empire—the third kingdom. This third kingdom was divided into four regions. Out of these regions—there were two that were most significant. One was in the Babylonian region, and the other was in Egypt. These kings are described as the kings of the North and the South.

The language being used for this little horn implies there is something demonic about him. The reader has perhaps observed a lot of similarity in these verses to the Antichrist in Revelation. This satanic individual takes away the daily sacrifice and sets up an abomination of desolation. This is also what the Antichrist does in the end times. Remember—the world works in cycles. There exists *prophetic cycles.*

I have mentioned this specific leader multiple times now in this chapter. This little horn is Antiochus Epiphanes. And he does many of the things the future Antichrist does—yet he existed prior to the first coming of Christ. He existed when the Grecian empire was effectively ruling the known world. This means we had an abomination of desolation even before Jesus Christ came to this earth. Verse 28 of Daniel 8 (which I provided at earlier) describes this leader as arising to power. This little horn arises in the latter part of the Grecian empire. He ruled before the Roman empire—but at the end of the Grecian empire. This man (Antiochus Epiphanes) is depicted as somebody in contact with dark forces. He recognizes dark sentences. He is mighty—but mighty because of the devil. *This little horn is a great foreshadowing of the future Antichrist.*

We have quite a lot of historical evidence of this Seleucid (one of the kingdoms of Grecia) ruler. Antiochus Epiphanes is described as magnifying himself. There have been coins unearthed that have his image on them. And these coins portray this man as being "God manifest". Antiochus Epiphanes claimed to be "God manifest". He is a type of antichrist. Since antichrist means "in the place of", and this man claimed to be God—he is a perfect example of a shadow fulfillment (with the main event taking place in the last days with the main Antichrist). Just like the future Antichrist—Antiochus Epiphanes is called the little horn, he takes away the daily sacrifice, and even sets up the abomination of desolation.

Isn't it noteworthy that we have two little horns? A little horn coming out of the fourth kingdom—and out of the Grecian kingdom? We have an antichrist even before the first coming of Jesus Christ, and an antichrist (the main Antichrist) in the end times, who will rule over the entire world under a one world kingdom. The end times Antichrist will fulfill all the details found in Daniel. Therefore, the futurist position is Biblical—while the preterist view of eschatology is false. The various forms of preterism are not reasonable, and this is especially true today in 2022 (as of the writing of this book). We can clearly see these same events described in Daniel 8 on the verge of coming true again—but on a more spectacular scale—or large scope. Don't be misled by preterists. They have a very unsophisticated view of end times theology. Yes—we've gotten many appetizers in terms of end times Bible prophecy—but we still have the main event—the **endgame.**

ALL WILL BE FULFILLED

We've already had an abomination of desolation with Antiochus Epiphanes. He took away the daily sacrifice. This all occurred in the Greek period of history. And even though this happened in the past—before the first coming of Jesus

123

Christ—Jesus makes it clear in Matthew 24 that there will be *another abomination of desolation in the future.* Jesus is obviously not talking about the abomination of desolation in the Greek period—He is talking about a future event. Then we go even further into the book of Revelation (the final book of the Bible) and we are still reading about the abomination of desolation (Revelation 13 with the image of the beast).

Earlier in this comprehensive chapter, we discussed dual-prophecy fulfillment. I pointed to several occurrences in scripture where we have immediate or partial fulfillment followed by the more dramatic future fulfillment. We've had more than one day of the Lord, but we will have a future day of the Lord (the main event). Babylon was destroyed even before the first coming of Jesus Christ. And yet the destruction of Babylon is still being talked about in Revelation. We have an antichrist in Daniel 7 and another one in Daniel 8. And yet both antichrists are separated by thousands of years. There are foreshadows of the great day of the Lord, and there are foreshadows of the Antichrist, his one world government, and the future abomination of desolation. An abomination of desolation is documented as having taken place in the past with Antiochus Epiphanes, and Jesus Christ speaks of another abomination of desolation in the future (dual-prophecy fulfillment). The world works in cycles, and it is of utmost importance that we do not forget this. Just because many of these events have happened in the past does not mean that these events are not pointing to something in the future.

Chapters 8 and 11 are a prime example of what I am talking about. The events in these chapters have all happened in the past. They happened—and they were a foreshadow of what's to come in the last days. We see the shadow fulfillment in these chapters—but *all* will be fulfilled in the future. Unfortunately, what we frequently see is a debate where both sides are arguing erroneously. Preterists claim everything has happened, and there is no application for the future. And many futurists (my position) want to say everything or nearly everything is only applying to future events—the last days. As futurists, we don't want to get stuck making arguments that the preterist can exploit. The truth is that both positions are true in many ways. Much of what we read about in the book of Daniel has happened (on a minor scale), and it will happen again (on a greater scale). We've had partial fulfillments and the foreshadowing of events to come. We also have the exact fulfillments awaiting in the future. We don't need to choose between Pepsi and coke—both are bad. Yes—futurism is true. But dual and triple-prophecy fulfillment is also true. Preterism and historicism are easy to refute—if we are refuting it in the proper way.

CHAPTER THREE

THE RAPTURE IN REVELATION

The Book of Revelation flows perfectly from the pre-wrath starting point. For example, we get the tribulation in chapters 6 and 13, and therefore should expect the rapture immediately following these chapters. *This is exactly what we find.* This is a confirmed expectation. We find the rapture in chapters 7 and 14 (right where we would expect them from the pre-wrath model of eschatology).

In Revelation chapter 14, we see Jesus with a sickle, and He is about to reap the earth. He gathers the elect—the believers. Jesus is gathering the wheat into His barn. Jesus is also coming on a cloud—just like we see in Matthew 24. In Matthew 24 we see Jesus coming in the clouds to gather His elect. And in Revelation 14—Jesus is on a cloud to reap the earth (gather the elect).

In chapter 14, we see God's wrath immediately following the rapture (another confirmed expectation). Remember—we have tribulation, rapture, and then God's wrath. And this is exactly what we find in the book of Revelation. It really is amazing just how consistent the pre-wrath position is.

In chapter 14, after Jesus reaps the earth, we see that mankind is about to enter the winepress of God's wrath. What does this mean exactly? Mankind (the unbelieving world) is about to face the intense wrath of God. Man's blood will be shed. All we must do is read about the events that transpire during the trumpets and the vials (representative of God's wrath). The trumpets and vials come after the seals. If we were to take all of the blood shed by man during this 3.5-year period and put it all into one place—it would fill up *"by the space of a thousand and six hundred furlongs."* The whole period of God's wrath is signified by *the winepress of the wrath of God.* Read from 14:20 to 15:1—it's obvious.

It is significant that we understand the proper chronology of Revelation. A proper understanding of the chronology of Revelation will help us fully comprehend what is going on here. Chapter 14 of Revelation fits in perfectly when we read it with the right chronology in mind. We see in chapters 1 to 11 the tribulation, 144,000 (discussed in detail later in this chapter), rapture, and then wrath. And in chapters 12 to 14 we see a going back in time (1st century AD to the birth of Christ with chapter 1 starting with John on the Isle of Patmos), tribulation, 144,000, rapture, and then wrath. Then we get the battle of Armageddon, the Millennium, and eventually the new heavens and new earth. Revelation 14 follows this sequence perfectly. Chapters 15 and 16 get into the 7 plagues of God's wrath—which correspond to God's wrath seen in chapters 8 through 11.

Matthew 13:39-43

[39] The enemy that sowed them is the devil; the harvest is the end of the world; and **the reapers are the angels**.

40 As therefore the tares are gathered and burned in the fire; so shall it be in the end of this world.

41 The Son of man shall send forth his angels, and they shall gather out of his kingdom all things that offend, and them which do iniquity;

42 And shall cast them into a furnace of fire: there shall be wailing and gnashing of teeth.

43 Then shall the righteous shine forth as the sun in the kingdom of their Father. Who hath ears to hear, let him hear.

What does Matthew 13:39-42 teach us about the rapture in Revelation 14?

- The reapers are the angels.

- The harvest is the end of the world.

- Regenerated believers are the wheat.

- Children of the devil are the tares or the weeds.

- Wheat goes into God's barn.

The pre-wrath position is once again validated by the scriptures. As expected, we have tribulation (Revelation 6 and 13), rapture (Revelation 7 and 14), and then God's wrath.

REVELATION 7—THE GREAT MULTITUDE

Both chapters (Revelation 7 and 14) have the rapture immediately after the tribulation (post-tribulation) and before God's wrath (pre-wrath). If Matthew 24, Luke 21, and Mark 13 teach that after the sun and moon are darkened, Jesus Christ comes in the clouds and the elect are caught up and gathered together—then we would no doubt expect to find this same event right after the sun and moon are found to be darkened in Revelation (which happens in Revelation 6). This is exactly what we find in Revelation 7.

Revelation 7:1

7 **And after these things** I saw four angels standing on the four corners of the earth, holding the four winds of the earth, that the wind should not blow on the earth, nor on the sea, nor on any tree.

I want the reader to observe Revelation 7:1 plainly stating the words "after these things." Revelation 7 fits in perfectly with the chronology of Revelation (Revelation 1-11 in complete chronological order followed by Revelation 12-22 being in perfect chronological order). This chapter is not outside of the timeline of Revelation—and specifically Revelation 1-11. The term "after these things" tells us chapter 7 picks up right where chapter 6 left off (with the sun and moon being darkened at the 6th seal).

Chapter 6 of the book of Revelation described the tribulation (including the great tribulation). The last thing discussed in Revelation 6 is the sun and moon being darkened. We also see the men of the earth crying and wailing because of the Lamb:

Revelation 6:15-17

¹⁵ And the kings of the earth, and the great men, and the rich men, and the chief captains, and the mighty men, and every bondman, and every free man, hid themselves in the dens and in the rocks of the mountains;

¹⁶ And said to the mountains and rocks, Fall on us, and hide us from the face of him that sitteth on the throne, and from the wrath of the Lamb:

¹⁷·**For the great day of his wrath is come; and who shall be able to stand?**

This perfect chronology should not be difficult to see—unless it does not want to be seen. Pre-tribulation rapturists must accuse the book of Revelation of being puzzling and difficult to understand. They must reject the chronology that has been laid out for us. They can't have the book of Revelation being understandable, because once it is recognized as being understandable, the pre-tribulation rapture must be discarded. We are told to be watchful, and to be ready for what's to come. Again—this is why the pre-tribulation rapture position makes no sense. The great day of His wrath is now here. This means God's wrath was not here prior to this event—which is because prior to Revelation 6, we were dealing with the tribulation, and not the wrath.

In verses 2 and 3 of Revelation chapter 7 we discover another important point:

Revelation 7:2-3

[2] And I saw another angel ascending from the east, having the seal of the living God: and he cried with a loud voice to the four angels, to whom it was given to hurt the earth and the sea,

[3] Saying, **Hurt not the earth, neither the sea, nor the trees, till we have sealed the servants of our God in their foreheads.**

The angel is saying not to hurt the earth, the sea, and the trees, until the servants of God are sealed in their foreheads. If God's wrath had already come—these verses would make no sense. In chapter 8 of Revelation—we see the start of the trumpet judgments (which come after the seals). These judgments represent God's wrath. Nothing prior to the trumpet judgments can then be considered God's wrath. If God's wrath was being poured out onto the earth, the earth, the sea, and the trees would obviously be hurt. They have not been hurt simply because God's wrath has not yet begun. The earth begins to be hurt in Revelation 8—where we see the earth and the sea starting to be devastated.

The wrath period does not begin until the 144,00 saved Israelites are sealed in heaven (to act as a witness during God's wrath period while believers who were raptured are in heaven). The 144,000 Israelite believers are sealed to be immune to the plagues of God's wrath. This is seen in verse 4 of Revelation 9:

Revelation 9:4

[4] And it was commanded them that they should not hurt the grass of the earth, neither any green thing, neither any tree; **but only those men which have not the seal of God in their foreheads.**

Unfortunately—there are many who hold to a strict post-tribulation rapture (not to be confused with the post-tribulation, pre-wrath position) who confuse the last trumpet judgment with the last trump of God at the rapture. Dr. Alan Kurshner adequately deals with this argument in **"Pre-Wrath Rapture: An Interview with Alan Kurschner."**

"**Post-tribulationists mistakenly interprets Paul's "last trump" with the seventh trumpet in the book of Revelation, consequently having the church on earth during God's wrath in the trumpet judgments**. In contrast, pre-wrath does not identify Paul's "last trump" with the seventh trumpet; instead, **pre-wrath interprets "last" (eschatos) in the specific context as "last" in the sense of signifying that the present order is no more, implying that a new era has dawned in God's redemptive work, which**

fits the resurrection context well in 1 Corinthians 15. In addition, eschatos can also carry the meaning of utmost or finest, which carries the connotation of culmination, again very fitting for the context in 1 Corinthians 15. Either of these latter senses is much more plausible than the post-tribulational interpretation of it referring to the seventh trumpet in the book of Revelation."

(Emphasis mine)

SOURCE: *Pre-Wrath Rapture: An Interview with Alan Kurschner.* (2013, December 2). My Digital Seminary. http://mydigitalseminary.com/pre-wrath-rapture-interview-alan-kurschner/

When the chronologies of Revelation are understood—there is no coherent way to argue the last trump is tantamount to the seventh trumpet judgment in the book of Revelation. This is because the seals come before the trumpet judgments and the rapture occurs at the sixth seal when the sun and moon are darkened. We still have God's wrath period after the rapture. The Millennium is not until after the battle of Armageddon (which is not to be mistaken with Matthew 24), which is after the seals, trumpets, and vials.

The reader will remember I mentioned a validated expectation based on the pre-wrath model of eschatology. This expectation is if Matthew 24 (God gathering together the elect after the sun and moon are darkened) really is the rapture—then the rapture should follow the sun and moon being darkened in Revelation 6. Remarkably—this is exactly what we find in verses 9-14 of Revelation 7:

Revelation 7:9-14

[9] After this I beheld, and, lo, **a great multitude**, which **no man could number**, of **all nations**, and kindreds, and people, and tongues, stood before the throne, and before the Lamb, clothed with white robes, and palms in their hands;

[10] And cried with a loud voice, saying, Salvation to our God which sitteth upon the throne, and unto the Lamb.

[11] And all the angels stood round about the throne, and about the elders and the four beasts, and fell before the throne on their faces, and worshipped God,

[12] Saying, Amen: Blessing, and glory, and wisdom, and thanksgiving, and honour, and power, and might, be unto our God for ever and ever. Amen.

[13] And one of the elders answered, saying unto me, **What are these which are arrayed in white robes? and whence came they?**

¹⁴ And I said unto him, Sir, thou knowest. And he said to me, These are they which came out **of great tribulation**, and have washed their robes, and made them white in the blood of the Lamb.

Just as expected—right after the sun and moon are darkened in Revelation 6—a great multitude than no man could number of all tribes, tongues, and nations, appear before the throne. This great multitude is said to be innumerable. There is no man that can number the amount of people appearing before the throne. This is obviously the rapture. The Bible has numbered some large numbers, and yet this is a number that no man could number. Not only that—but this is a great multitude that is instantaneously appearing before the throne. This would be expected if it were the rapture—rather than "tribulation saints". Pre-tribulation rapturists would have us believe that this great multitude represents newly converted saints during the tribulation period after believers have been raptured. This is a very weak argument. If this were the case—we would not be seeing a great multitude that no man could number appearing instantly before the throne. No—we would be seeing a gradual appearance of believers before the throne. It would be an accumulation of people appearing—since there would be differing numbers of Christians being martyred on the earth. Different amounts of Christians would be getting killed at different times during the tribulation period (according to the pre-tribulation rapture explanation of Revelation 7). It would not be a great multitude killed all at once. This pre-tribulation rapture rescue device has been falsified. It doesn't work.

In addition to this fatal blow to the pre-tribulation rapture interpretation of the great multitude—it doesn't fit the chronology. The chronology indicates that the great multitude is definitely the rapture, because it associates perfectly and reliably with the elect being gathered together in Matthew 24 (after the tribulation and when the sun and moon are darkened).

Understanding the chronology of the book of Revelation makes the book flow consistently. The chronology is clear, and the chronology alone is enough to demonstrate the strength of the pre-wrath position. It is also enough to prove how inconsistent the pre-tribulation rapture model is (as well as other false eschatological positions). Chapters 6 and 13 record the events of the tribulation. Chapter 7 has the 144,000 saved Israelites (resurrected Old Testament saints) being sealed for immunity to God's wrath. Then we see (also in chapter 7) a great multitude appearing in heaven (this great multitude comprises believers of all nations and kindreds). This great multitude that no man could number is said to have come out of great tribulation (fitting perfectly with Matthew 24, Luke 21, and Mark 13). Chapter 7 also makes it clear that this great multitude has *just* arrived. They appear promptly before the throne. In chapter 8, God's wrath begins (represented by the trumpet judgments). Then chapter 11 ends with the Millennium (the kingdoms of this world have become the kingdoms of Jesus Christ).

We still have chapters 12-22. The chronology of Revelation starts over in chapter 12. We know this because we are taken all the way back in time to the birth of Christ. Following chapter 12, we are given all of the same events from chapters 1-11 again. The tribulation is described in chapter 13 (mark of the beast, one world government, one world religion, and the great image). Then as expected, we get the 144,000, and the rapture immediately following the tribulation in chapter 13. The 144,000 and the rapture are covered in chapter 14. After the rapture, we get (as expected again) the pouring out of God's wrath (vials). I pray the reader can clearly see how consistent this is.

Pre-tribulation rapturists cannot explain why the pre-wrath model is so consistent. We start in the 1st century AD (John on the Isle of Patmos in Revelation 1 and the birth of Jesus Christ in Revelation 12), the tribulation period, the sealing of the 144,000, the rapture, and then God's wrath. The chronologies are very reliably coherent in the first half of Revelation and the second half. In the second half we get additional details in terms of what occurs at the Millennium and after (battle of Gog and Magog, new heavens and new earth).

The reader has probably noticed just how similar chapters 7 and 14 are to each other (as expected given the chronology of Revelation explained thoroughly in this book). Both chapters have the 144,000 sealed Israelites and also the rapture (great multitude in Revelation 7 and Jesus on a white cloud reaping the harvest of the earth in Revelation 14). Revelation 7 and 14 are also located right in between the tribulation (Revelation 6 and 13) and God's wrath (Revelation

8, 15, and 16). We should see by now why Revelation means "to be revealed". God wants us to understand these things. This is why I found this book to be incredibly important to write. I want to show just how consistent end times theology is when interpreted from the correct starting point. Anybody who is saved should be able to pick up the Bible and read Revelation for themselves to see exactly what I am describing.

I want to point out that the 144,000 Israelites are already sealed by the time the rapture takes place. The 144,000 are ready to be put on the earth to act as a witness to the lost while God pours out His wrath. God never leaves the earth without a witness. God always has righteous men and women on the earth to preach the Gospel and save the lost. This is why the 144,000, and the 2 witnesses, are so important in end times theology.

The 144,000 saved Israelites are with the Lamb (Jesus Christ) in heaven. This is when they are sealed according to the scriptures. We know this because the Lamb is on Mount Zion. Mount Zion is located in the heavenly Jerusalem. Hebrews 12:22 describes the heavenly Jerusalem where Mount Zion is located. At this point in time (in Revelation), Jesus Christ is in heaven, and since the 144,000 Israelites are with the Lamb on Mount Zion, they are in heaven, and not on earth. We see this in both Revelation 7 and 14. John is hearing the voices of singers and harpers located in heaven. These voices are singing a song before the throne (in heaven), which is the same heavenly scene described in Revelation chapters 4 and 5. Verse 3 of Revelation 14 makes it clear that no man could learn the song being sung by those singing in heaven, except for the 144,000 Israelites. This entire scene is in heaven. Revelation 14 makes it clear that the sealing of the 144,000 takes place in heaven. This makes sense because this is all before the pouring out of God's wrath (trumpets and vials). The 144,000 will then be sent to earth, after they are sealed. They will be located on earth during the wrath period. I find it very interesting that the 144,000 are sealed in heaven at the beginning of Revelation 7, and also at the beginning of Revelation 14. Then we have the rapture occurring at the end of Revelation 7 and the end of Revelation 14. There is a perfect order of events being described here. If the 144,000 Israelites are being sealed before the rapture (Jesus Christ coming in the clouds to gather together His elect), then that means they must be in heaven. How does a believer make it to heaven prior to the rapture? The answer is simple. They must die. A believer who dies is immediately in heaven. Paul says to be *absent from the body is to be present with the Lord.* When a regenerate believer dies, their regenerated spirit goes to heaven, and their unregenerate body goes into the ground. *This means the 144,000 saved Israelites are resurrected Old Testament saints.* These saints will preach the Gospel while believers who were caught up at the rapture are in heaven preparing to come back for the battle of Armageddon (which occurs after God's wrath). The topic of the 144,000 will be expanded on later in this chapter.

THE BODY AND THE EAGLES

We get an excellent picture of the rapture in verses 26-28 of Matthew 24:

Matthew 24:26-28

²⁶ Wherefore if they shall say unto you, Behold, he is in the desert; go not forth: behold, he is in the secret chambers; believe it not.

²⁷ For as the lightning cometh out of the east, and shineth even unto the west; so shall also the coming of the Son of man be.

²⁸ For wheresoever the carcase is, there will the eagles be gathered together.

Many have unfortunately misunderstood this passage. It has been argued this is a negative gathering. But what we actually see here is a positive one. The carcass in verse 28 is singular—and the eagles are plural. This makes sense when you understand Jesus (singular) represents the carcass (since Jesus will be in the clouds), and the eagles represent believers—since eagles are in the plural form. The coming of the Son of man will be like eagles gathering together at a carcass. This makes perfect sense. Jesus Christ comes in the clouds—and the elect are gathered to meet Him in the air. Jesus is the carcass, and we are the eagles since we are the ones gathering to Jesus. I am flabbergasted at how many people miss this. Those that hold to the amillennialism and postmillennialism positions especially butcher this one. Remember—amillennialists and postmillennialists lack a consistent model. They are forced to reject the 2-chronology structure of Revelation. They essentially isolate random verses in Revelation and make up their own out-of-order timeline.

Critics will argue "but eagles gathering to eat a carcass promotes negative thoughts." Basically—these critics see this as a negative picture—rather than a positive one. They miss the obvious (what should be obvious) point that eagles gathering around a carcass is in fact perceived by the eagles as a plentiful meal. A bountiful meal is a wonderful thing for eagles. And Jesus Christ coming in the clouds to gather His elect is also a wonderful event. As a matter of fact—this is what we wait for! This is the redemption of our bodies. Those that hold to pretribulationism must reject this factual interpretation simply because many of them are forced to argue that the rapture is not talked about in Matthew 24. Some have gone as far as saying the rapture is not talked about at all in the Gospels—and is basically not brought up until Paul. This is absurd and unsupported by the scriptures—as I have proven in this book. We find the Great Commision and the Last Supper in the Gospel of Matthew. Are we to believe that these are not for followers of Jesus Christ? If pre-tribulation rapturists were consistent (which they clearly aren't), they'd argue the Great Commision and the Last Supper are also written specifically for "Israel". Jesus Christ is talking to His followers in Matthew 24, not unsaved Jews.

Notice the imagery used in Exodus 19:4 to signify believers being brought to God:

Exodus 19:4

[4] Ye have seen what I did unto the Egyptians, **and how I bare you on eagles' wings, and brought you unto myself.**

There is no debate on this matter. Jesus Christ is the carcass, and the elect (believers/saints) are the eagles. This is a symbolic representation of the rapture—of believers being gathered together with Jesus Christ in the clouds. This is not a negative gathering—this is in fact a positive one that pre-tribulation rapturists have not adequately dealt with. This isn't the first time Jesus uses comparable symbolism and imagery:

John 6:53

[53] Then Jesus said unto them, Verily, verily, I say unto you, **Except ye eat the flesh of the Son of man, and drink his blood, ye have no life in you.**

Luke 17 further strengthens this interpretation:

Luke 17:34-37

[34] I tell you, in that night there shall be **two men in one bed; the one shall be taken, and the other shall be left.**

[35] Two women shall be grinding together; the one shall be taken, and the other left.

[36] Two men shall be in the field; the one shall be taken, and the other left.

[37] And they answered and said unto him, Where, Lord? And he said unto them,

Wheresoever the body is, thither will the eagles be gathered together.

What we see here in these verses are people being taken and others being left behind. This is a clear-cut reference to the rapture. Since this world is a combination of believers and unbelievers—the rapture will be made up of many people being taken—and others being left behind to withstand God's wrath. For example: if you are a believer, and work with unbelievers—if the rapture were to take place while you were working—you'd be taken—and your unsaved coworkers will be left behind. It makes perfect sense that since verses 34-36 are a picture of the rapture—verse 37 would be as well. Jesus Christ is giving us an anticipated picture of what will happen when He comes in the clouds to gather His elect. He illustrates this amazing event as eagles gathering to the body. In Matthew—Jesus used a carcass to symbolize Himself in the clouds—and in Luke, He used a body. On both occasions—believers are represented or symbolized as eagles. This could not be clearer.

REVELATION 4:1 IS NOT THE RAPTURE

Pre-tribulation rapturists require a rapture prior to Revelation 6—since Revelation 6 is clearly describing events associated with the tribulation. Proponents of the pre-tribulation rapture want the rapture prior to the tribulation—even though Matthew 24 clearly says the rapture (Christ coming in the clouds) is after (not before) the tribulation. Some have looked to Revelation 4:1 as being the rapture. They will say John on the Isle of Patmos being taken up into heaven (spiritually—not bodily) is symbolic of the "church" being caught up at the rapture:

Revelation 4:1

4 After this I looked, and, behold, a door was opened in heaven: **and the first voice which I heard was as it were of a trumpet talking with me**; which said, **Come up hither**, and **I will shew thee things which must be hereafter.**

This argument is weak, and has no evidential support. But for a moment—let us assume this argument is valid. If pre-tribulation rapturists are consistent in this line of reasoning, they will still be forced to conclude the rapture is after the tribulation:

Revelation 1:9

[9]**I John, who also am your brother, and companion in tribulation**, and in the kingdom and patience of Jesus Christ, was in the isle that is called Patmos, for the word of God, and for the testimony of Jesus Christ.

If pre-tribulation rapturists want to take Revelation 4:1 as being symbolic of the rapture, then to be consistent, they would have to admit that Revelation 1:9 indicates the rapture is after the tribulation—since John states he is in tribulation. Even a symbolic interpretation of Revelation 4:1 is more consistent within a post-tribulation, pre-wrath rapture position.

Pre-tribulation rapturists are not consistent though. They are forced to take Revelation 4:1 as being symbolic of the rapture and reject Revelation 1:9 as reflecting the proper ordering of end times events. If we are to assume their Revelation 4:1 argument is legit—then we have to admit that Revelation 1:9 is teaching tribulation prior to the rapture. Either way you look at it—there is no help for the pre-tribulation rapture.

Now I want to prove that Revelation 4:1 is not to be taken as symbolic—and is literally referring to John being taken up in spirit to be shown things in heaven and things to come. Firstly—we have seen that even if we assume the validity of the pre-tribulation rapturists argument—it doesn't work (since John is in tribulation in Revelation 1:9). Let us examine Revelation 4:1 in detail:

Revelation 4:1-2

4 After this I looked, and, behold, a door was opened in heaven: and the **first voice** which I heard was **as it were of a trumpet** talking with me; which said, Come up hither, and I will shew thee things which must be hereafter.

² And **immediately I was in the spirit**: and, behold, a throne was set in heaven, and one sat on the throne.

Once again—Pre-tribulation advocates need a rapture prior to the tribulation (which is found in Chapter 6). This is the best they have come up with. Here are some of the aspects of Revelation 4:1 that tell us clearly this is not the rapture of all believers of all time up to this point:

- One man being called up (not the rapture).

The rapture is all believers of all ages (the dead in Christ, those that are alive and remain). This would be a great multitude that no man could number (an innumerable multitude). A single man is not the Rapture.

- One man being caught up spiritually.

The rapture is a bodily resurrection. Believers will be glorified (final sanctification) and receive new bodies. This is not described in Revelation 4:1.

- A voice like a trumpet.

The rapture consists of a trumpet—not a voice **LIKE** a trumpet. A voice "like" a trumpet is talking about the **VOLUME** of the voice.

Isaiah 58:1

58 Cry aloud, spare not, lift up thy **voice like a trumpet**, and shew my people their transgression, and the house of Jacob their sins.

John is simply saying he heard a loud voice. A voice with the volume like a trumpet is not a trumpet sounding (this should be obvious).

Revelation 4:1 has no mention of Jesus Christ coming in the clouds. When John is caught up and taken to heaven, Jesus is there seated at the right hand of the Father. We see no evidence of Jesus Christ descending, coming in the clouds, and gathering together His elect (having believers meet Him in the air). There is no mention of John meeting the Lord in the air. What we have in Revelation 4:1 (which according to pre-tribulation rapturists is the rapture):

- One man (John on the Isle of Patmos), no trumpet, no clouds, and no Jesus Christ coming in the clouds to gather the elect.

- John was not bodily or physically caught up to heaven in Revelation 4:1-2. Again—the rapture will be a bodily resurrection. Those that are alive and remain will be caught up physically to meet Him in the clouds where we receive a new glorified body. The rapture is a physical occurrence.

- This passage has nothing at all in common with the rapture.

- A man caught up in spirit (not even bodily) rather than an innumerable multitude (Revelation 7) makes it clear this verse is **NOT** the rapture. End of story.

In the Bible—there are many occurrences where men are carried to heaven spiritually—not physically. This is what we are seeing in Revelation 4:1. Basically—John is being caught up spiritually to be shown things which must come to pass.

Ezekiel 37:1

37 The hand of the Lord was upon me, and
carried me out in the spirit of the Lord, and set
me down in the midst of the valley which was
full of bones,

Being taken up to heaven spiritually means the body stays
where it is. This is similar to what is called a trance. It should
be obvious to anybody that being caught up in the spirit and
shown important things is not the same thing as a bodily
resurrection at the rapture.

Pre-tribulation promoters must literally believe that the
only place in the entire book of Revelation the rapture is
mentioned in Revelation 4:1-2 (one man being caught up in
the spirit). If you can swallow this as being even remotely
convincing and realistic—then you may just be a solid
candidate for believing in the pre-tribulation rapture. And this
is a great step in believing the pre-tribulation rapture because
there are a great multitude of other things just like this that
you will have to ignore reality to believe.

Revelation 7:9-14

⁹ After this I beheld, and, lo, **a great multitude**,
which **no man could number**, of **all nations**,
and kindreds, and people, and tongues, stood
before the throne, and before the Lamb, clothed
with white robes, and palms in their hands;

¹⁰ And cried with a loud voice, saying,
Salvation to our God which sitteth upon the
throne, and unto the Lamb.

¹¹ And all the angels stood round about the throne, and about the elders and the four beasts, and fell before the throne on their faces, and worshipped God,

¹² Saying, Amen: Blessing, and glory, and wisdom, and thanksgiving, and honour, and power, and might, be unto our God for ever and ever. Amen.

¹³ And one of the elders answered, saying unto me, **What are these which are arrayed in white robes? and whence came they?**

¹⁴ And I said unto him, Sir, thou knowest. And he said to me, These are they which came out **of great tribulation**, and have washed their robes, and made them white in the blood of the Lamb.

I discussed Revelation 7 and the great multitude earlier in this chapter. This great multitude comprises a number of individuals that no man could number. It is a massive group that has come out of great tribulation and it is obviously the rapture. This great multitude suddenly appears in heaven after the tribulation (described in Revelation 6 with the opening of the seals) and after the sun and moon go dark. This series of events fits perfectly. We see tribulation, sun and moon darkened, rapture, great multitude appearing in heaven, and wrath.

Isn't a **GREAT MULTITUDE** that **NO MAN COULD NUMBER** much more consistent with the rapture than Revelation 4:1 (one guy being caught up spiritually and not even bodily)? As expected—right after the sun and moon are darkened—a great multitude that no man could number (the Bible has numbered some very large numbers) promptly appears in Heaven. An important question is asked at the end of Revelation 7: "**What are these which are arrayed in white robes? and whence came they?**" And the answer is provided: "**These are they which came out of great tribulation, and have washed their robes, and made them white in the blood of the Lamb.**"

If the post-tribulation, pre-wrath rapture is not true—then *why do all these passages fit so perfectly in this eschatological model?* The pre-tribulation rapturists that refuse to admit the rapture comes after the tribulation, and before God's wrath, must essentially argue this is all a giant coincidence. And yet—the pre-tribulation rapturists are incapable of pointing out the rapture in Revelation (even though the book of Revelation has been written in order that end times events can be revealed, and understood). There are those that do point to a verse in Revelation as apparently being the rapture—using Revelation 4:1—and we have covered extensively as to why Revelation 4:1 is clearly not the rapture.

John was taken up temporarily and did not actually be forever with the Lord. As a matter of fact—John's body never left the Isle of Patmos. His body never moved. It stayed exactly where it was. He was taken up into heaven spiritually. Therefore, if we take Revelation 4:1 as the rapture—we have to say that the rapture is temporary. John was only caught up momentarily—but the actual rapture consists of believers staying with the Lord eternally—and then coming back with the Lord during the battle in Armageddon (which is after the tribulation and wrath). We will stay with the Lord always after the rapture. Forever we will be with the Lord.

We have both Revelation 7 and 14 that fit perfectly with the rapture (1 Thessalonians 4). Revelation 7 is an innumerable multitude. And this innumerable multitude appears in heaven after the sun and moon darkened, and right before God's wrath. Jesus comes in a cloud to reap the harvest of the earth in Revelation 14 after the tribulation (Revelation 13) and right before God's wrath. This fits a lot better than Revelation 4:1, and this is because Revelation 4:1 is not the rapture. The pre-tribulation rapture is bankrupt. As a matter of fact—less and less people are taking this position seriously. It is so obviously false—and the more we see the last days (Daniel's 70th week) approaching—the more people are waking up to the truth of the end times. The truth is the post-tribulation, pre-wrath rapture. Believers will be here for the dawn of the Antichrist. And believers must be prepared for this time of tribulation and persecution. But do not fear, we will be rescued out of this earth right before God's wrath is poured down upon the wicked unbelieving world.

THE 24 ELDERS

Proponents of a pre-tribulation rapture have argued for their position by pointing to the 24 elders in Revelation 4:

Revelation 4:10-11

[10] **The four and twenty elders** fall down
before him that sat on the throne, and worship
him that liveth for ever and ever, and cast their
crowns before the throne, saying,

[11] Thou art worthy, O Lord, to receive glory and
honour and power: for thou hast created all
things, and for thy pleasure they are and were
created.

In the Bible—elder is used synonymously with the
word bishop or pastor. Therefore, these 24 elders essentially
represent pastors or bishops. Since these 24 elders are seen in
heaven prior to the opening of the 1st seal, and hence the
tribulation, pre-tribulation rapturists have attempted to argue
for a rapture prior to the tribulation. This is another prime
example of the circular reasoning defenders of
pretribulationism are guilty of. There has not been any
mention of the rapture up to this point in the book of
Revelation. But pre-tribulation rapturists know they need a
rapture prior to Revelation 6 when the seals begin to be
opened. I have already debunked the unscriptural and illogical
argument that Revelation 4:1 is the rapture (one man being
caught up in spirit) and this argument isn't any better. As a
matter of fact—both of these arguments are easily refuted.

Basically, pretribbers claim (without evidence) that the
24 elders represent the "church" and are therefore not literally
24 elders/pastors. And for those that admit these are literally
24 people, they will argue for a rapture prior to the tribulation

simply because we have saved people in heaven prior to revelation 6. These arguments have obviously not been thought through very well. Millions of believers are in heaven right now. Does this mean the rapture has already taken place? Of course not. Paul says once we die—we are immediately with the Lord in heaven:

2 Corinthians 5:8

8 We are confident, I say, and willing rather to be absent from the body, and to be present with the Lord.

Arguing for a pre-tribulation rapture simply because Revelation 4 mentions 24 elders in heaven doesn't prove anything. Everybody who is saved and has died is present in heaven. Believers have not yet been glorified (final sanctification) because the rapture has not yet occurred—but believers' regenerate spirits are in heaven. When you got saved—you were passed from death unto life—from a state of un-regeneration to regeneration. This regeneration took place spiritually. Nothing changed about your unregenerate flesh in the moment of salvation. Remember—as believers—we are waiting for the redemption of our bodies. Therefore, when a believer dies, their unregenerate flesh goes into the ground, and the regenerated spirit goes to heaven. This means believers have gone to heaven long before the rapture. Even apologists of the pre-tribulation rapture will admit the rapture hasn't happened yet. And so why use such a weak argument for their position? The answer is simple. They must have a rapture prior to the tribulation that starts in Revelation 6. Unfortunately for them—there is no rapture mentioned prior to Revelation 7. The rapture does occur in Revelation—but it doesn't occur until Revelation 7 and 14—both of which are right after the tribulation—and before God's wrath. This is exactly what a pre-wrath rapturist would predict. The pre-wrath model is consistent and sophisticated—and the pre-tribulation view of eschatology lacks both consistency and sophistication.

Pre-tribulation advocates have also pointed to the crowns and white clothing of the 24 elders:

Revelation 4:4

⁴ And round about the throne were four and twenty seats: and upon the seats I saw four and twenty elders sitting, **clothed in white raiment**; and **they had on their heads crowns of gold.**

They will say the 24 elders must be in heaven due to the rapture since their descriptions fit that of physical bodies. But this also doesn't work and I can prove this from Revelation 6:

Revelation 6:9-11

⁹ And when he had opened the fifth seal, **I saw under the altar the souls of them that were slain for the word of God, and for the testimony which they held:**

¹⁰ And they cried with a loud voice, saying, How long, O Lord, holy and true, dost thou not

judge and avenge our blood on them that dwell on the earth?

[11] **And white robes were given unto every one of them**; and it was said unto them, that they should rest yet for a little season, until their fellowservants also and their brethren, that should be killed as they were, should be fulfilled.

Just because the 24 elders have crowns and are wearing white raiment does not mean their bodies have been resurrected. We see distinctly in Revelation 6 that the souls (not glorified resurrected bodies) are pictured as having white robes. The souls first mentioned in verse 9 of Revelation 6 were killed during the tribulation. They are said to have been slain for the word of God. And even though the rapture has not yet occurred (since it occurs after the sun and moon go dark in Revelation 6), meaning they have not yet been given new bodies, they have white robes. Therefore, the presence of 24 elders in heaven prior to Revelation 6 does not prove a pre-tribulation rapture. This is grasping at straws. Dr. Alan Kurschner makes several excellent points on this topic:

> "Pretribulationism frequently asserts that the 24 elders represent the raptured church because they were dressed in white and had crowns on their head. **But white is a color that simply represents purity, so it is a strained reading to require this to be the raptured church. Further, crowns are not exclusive to believers. Christ has a crown (Rev 14:14).**

155

Even angelic-demons is said to wear something like crowns (Rev 9:7). The first seal rider who very well may represent Antichrist, or false christs, has a crown (Rev 6:2).

What is weak about this interpretation is that if the raptured church is suppose to be in heaven at this time, and the focus is on the *lamb* **of God who gave his life for this church, we are given no hint of any great multitude in this scene. Moreover, why should there be a representation of the church by the elders if in fact the reality of the church is present? And suppose the 24 elders do represent, for example, the 12 tribes of Israel and the 12 disciples who represent true Israel and the true church respectively, why would that require the rapture to have happened before that scene?**

So we should avoid reading a theological premise into an unclear verse or entity. And as it is often sagaciously said about this passage: Our attention should be drawn to the worshipped One, not the worshippers."

(Emphasis mine)

SOURCE: *Do the Twenty Four Elders "Represent" the Church?* (2012, January 23). ESCHATOS MINISTRIES.

THE 144,000

At the end of chapter 6 of Revelation, the sun and moon were darkened, the stars fell from heaven, and the men of the earth were bracing themselves for the wrath of God. We enter Revelation 7 where the angels are waiting for the wrath to be poured out through the trumpet judgments:

Revelation 7:2-5

² And I saw another angel ascending from the east, having the seal of the living God: and he cried with a loud voice to the four angels, to whom it was given to hurt the earth and the sea,

³ Saying, **Hurt not the earth, neither the sea, nor the trees, till we have sealed the servants of our God in their foreheads.**

⁴ And I heard the number of them which were sealed: and there were sealed an hundred and forty and four thousand of all the tribes of the children of Israel.

⁵ Of the tribe of Juda were sealed twelve thousand. Of the tribe of Reuben were sealed twelve thousand. Of the tribe of Gad were sealed twelve thousand.

In Revelation 7, the earth is about to be devastated. But before this happens—there is a short period where the servants of God need to be sealed. We have a very consistent flow of events up to this point. This sealing is taking place right in between the sixth seal of chapter 6 and the 7th seal in Revelation 7. Everything has paused to seal the servants that will be placed onto the earth during God's wrath—which is why the wrath has not yet begun. These 144,000 are from the 12 tribes of the children of Israel (12,000 of each tribe):

Revelation 7:4-8

[4] And I heard the number of them which were sealed: and there were sealed **an hundred and forty and four thousand of all the tribes of the children of Israel**.

[5] **Of the tribe of Juda were sealed twelve thousand**. **Of the tribe of Reuben were sealed twelve thousand**. **Of the tribe of Gad were sealed twelve thousand**.

[6] **Of the tribe of Aser were sealed twelve thousand**. **Of the tribe of Nephthalim were sealed twelve thousand**. **Of the tribe of Manasses were sealed twelve thousand.**

[7] **Of the tribe of Simeon were sealed twelve thousand**. **Of the tribe of Levi were sealed twelve thousand**. **Of the tribe of Issachar were sealed twelve thousand**.

**⁸ Of the tribe of Zabulon were sealed twelve
thousand. Of the tribe of Joseph were sealed
twelve thousand. Of the tribe of Benjamin
were sealed twelve thousand.**

This is obviously a literal number. We know this
because God is taking the time to give us the specific details
of these 144,000—which comprises 12,000 from each tribe.
God takes several verses to explain this. If this were just a
figurative or symbolic number—this would be unnecessary.
These are real numbers, and not just figurative ones.

After God gives us the specific numbers of the
144,000, chapter 7 moves into the great multitude that appear
in heaven (the rapture):

Revelation 7:9-12

⁹ After this I beheld, and, lo, **a great multitude,
which no man could number, of all nations**,
and **kindreds, and people**, and **tongues**, stood
before the throne, and before the Lamb, clothed
with white robes, and palms in their hands;

¹⁰ And cried with a loud voice, saying,
Salvation to our God which sitteth upon the
throne, and unto the Lamb.

¹¹ And all the angels stood round about the
throne, and about the elders and the four beasts,
and fell before the throne on their faces, and
worshipped God,

¹² Saying, Amen: Blessing, and glory, and wisdom, and thanksgiving, and honour, and power, and might, be unto our God for ever and ever. Amen.

As expected from the pre-wrath model of eschatology—we have the tribulation, then the sealing of the 144,000, the rapture, and the start of God's wrath. This makes perfect sense since God wants a witness on this earth while He pours out His wrath on the wicked. But since His wrath is going to be poured out during this time—the witnesses, or soulwinners, need to be sealed and protected from these plagues.

The next mention of the 144,000 is in Revelation 9 (which is describing the events of God's wrath):

Revelation 9:1-4

9 And the fifth angel sounded, and I saw a star fall from heaven unto the earth: and to him was given the key of the bottomless pit.

² And he opened the bottomless pit; and there arose a smoke out of the pit, as the smoke of a great furnace; and the sun and the air were darkened by reason of the smoke of the pit.

³ And there came out of the smoke locusts upon the earth: and unto them was given power, as the scorpions of the earth have power.

⁴ And it was commanded them that they should not hurt the grass of the earth, neither any green thing, neither any tree; **but only those men which have not the seal of God in their foreheads.**

The reader will remember how chapter 7 of Revelation started out with a pause in heaven—where God did not want the earth hurt just yet. This was because He wanted His servants sealed first. This also tells us God's wrath has not yet started—nor have the trumpet judgments taken place (refuting those that want to say the trumpets happen prior to the sun and moon darkening, and the rapture). Now that the 144,000 are sealed in chapter 7, and the great multitude has appeared in heaven, God begins to pour out His wrath (as the 7 trumpets are sounded) in chapters 8 and 9. We see fire and brimstone raining down from heaven, the water is turned into blood, and men are being scorched with great heat. Notice how these are all supernatural events—while the seals involved primarily man made events. In the seals—the tribulation—we saw war and then the ripple effect of war. But during God's wrath—we see supernatural events. We see plagues. In chapter 9, the bottomless pit is opened, and these terrifying locusts come out of hell to torment the men that dwell on the earth. We see this specifically in verse 3. It is the 144,000 that cannot be hurt by the locusts (a judgment of God). As men are suffering the wrath of God, the 144,000 are immune to this judgment. The locusts cannot hurt them.

We can see that at the time of God's wrath—the 144,000 are now on the earth. They are immune from the wrath being poured out onto the earth. Interestingly—we see a foreshadowing of this in Ezekiel where anybody with the mark on their foreheads are spared from judgment:

Ezekiel 9:4-7

[4] And the Lord said unto him, Go through the midst of the city, through the midst of Jerusalem, and **set a mark upon the foreheads of the men that sigh and that cry for all the abominations that be done in the midst thereof.**

[5] And **to the others he said in mine hearing, Go ye after him through the city, and smite: let not your eye spare, neither have ye pity:**

[6] Slay utterly old and young, both maids, and little children, and women: but come not near any man upon whom is the mark; and begin at my sanctuary. Then they began at the ancient men which were before the house.

[7] And he said unto them, Defile the house, and fill the courts with the slain: go ye forth. And they went forth, and slew in the city.

The third and final place where the 144,000 are mentioned is in Revelation 14 (which is located in the second chronological section of Revelation):

Revelation 14:1-5

14 And I looked, and, lo, **a Lamb stood on the mount Sion, and with him an hundred forty and four thousand,** having his Father's name written in their foreheads.

² And I **heard a voice from heaven,** as the **voice of many waters,** and as **the voice of a great thunder:** and **I heard the voice of harpers harping with their harps:**

³ And **they** sung as it were a new song before the throne, and **before the four beasts,** and the elders: and **no man could learn that song but the hundred and forty and four thousand, which were redeemed from the earth.**

⁴ **These are they which were not defiled with women; for they are virgins. These are they which follow the Lamb whithersoever he goeth. These were redeemed from among men, being the firstfruits unto God and to the Lamb.**

⁵ And in their mouth was found no guile: for they are without fault before the throne of God.

The first thing I want the reader to notice is the location of the 144,000 in Revelation 14. We clearly see the 144,000 are in heaven. They are with the Lamb and the Lamb stands on mount Sion. This is not an earthly mount Sion. We see an earthly mountain in the Old Testament—just like there exists an earthly or physical Jerusalem. We know there exists both a heavenly mount Sion, and an earthly mount Sion. There exists both an earthly Jerusalem and a heavenly Jerusalem (that is made up of all believers). The heavenly mount Sion is associated with the heavenly Jerusalem:

Hebrews 12:22-24

²² But ye are come unto **mount Sion**, and unto **the city of the living God**, **the heavenly Jerusalem**, and to an innumerable company of angels,

²³ To the general assembly and church of the firstborn, which are written in heaven, and to God the Judge of all, and to the spirits of just men made perfect,

²⁴ And to Jesus the mediator of the new covenant, and to the blood of sprinkling, that speaketh better things than that of Abel.

According to Revelation 14, there is a song being sung that only the 144,000 can sing. If we hear this song, it must be the 144,000 singing it. These verses in Revelation 14 are clear. I urge the reader to read through them carefully. The sound of the song is coming from heaven. Since the 144,000 are the ones singing the song, the 144,000 must be in heaven. Verse 3 clearly says this song is being sung before the throne. This is how we know the mount Sion being referred to is the heavenly one. The 144,000 are with the lamb, they are on mount Sion, and the song they are singing is a song only they can learn and know. This is a scene clearly occurring in heaven. The end of verse 3 makes this even more clear. We learn these 144,000 Israelites were redeemed from the earth. This tells us this group are saints in heaven that got to heaven by dying.

We also learn in Revelation 14 that the 144,000 are all male virgins. They had not defiled themselves with women. They are also said to be without fault. This is yet another reason why we know they are in heaven. If this group were on earth, and in the flesh, they could not appropriately be referred to as having no fault. The 144,000 have no fault, and are found to be in heaven, because they are regenerate believers who have already physically died and made their way to heaven. When we got saved—it was our spirit that was regenerated—and not our flesh. Remember—we still look for the redemption of our bodies. When we die as believers, our flesh goes into the ground, and our perfect and sinless regenerated spirits go to heaven. We will be without fault—just like the 144,000. The only reason we struggle with sin on this earth is because we still have this unregenerate flesh. Paul talks about the daily battle between the flesh and the spirit—or the old man and the new man.

What do we know so far?

- This group was redeemed from the earth,

- It consists of 12,000 Israelites from the tribes of the children of Israel,

- They are all male,

- They are all virgin.

The typical teaching you will find from most Bible interpreters is a very generalized, nonliteral, and sloppy interpretation. I am taking these passages at face value. These are also clearly not all Jews—and therefore it is also erroneous to call this group "144,000 Jews". Many of the tribes listed are not Jews (for example: the tribe of Reuben). A Jew is someone from the Southern Kingdom of Judah. The first time the word "Jew" is used in the Bible is in 2 Kings:

2 Kings 16:5-7

[5] Then Rezin king of Syria and Pekah son of Remaliah king of Israel came up to Jerusalem to war: and they besieged Ahaz, but could not overcome him.

[6] At that time Rezin king of Syria recovered Elath to Syria, and **drave the Jews from Elath**: and the Syrians came to Elath, and dwelt there unto this day.

[7] So Ahaz sent messengers to Tiglathpileser king of Assyria, saying, I am thy servant and thy son: come up, and save me out of the hand of the king of Syria, and out of the hand of the king of Israel, which rise up against me.

It's quite interesting to see just how many Bible interpreters are guilty of overgeneralizing things. It is important that we understand Biblical truths according to their appropriate time period. When God mentions a word for the first time, we will often find a definition of that word. In this passage, the northern Kingdom of Israel has teamed up with Syria for war against the southern kingdom of Judah. Syria and Israel work together as allies in their fight against Judah.

I want to be as careful and consistent as possible. As somebody who is writing this book, I want to ensure that I am providing the most coherent teachings possible with comprehensive and sophisticated interpretations of God's Word. This is why I will not do what many Bible interpreters do (pre-wrath rapturists are also guilty of this faulty understanding of the 144,000) and simply say "the 144,000 are 144,000 Jews."

A Jew is contrasted with Israel in the same way somebody from California (Californian) is contrasted with America. We have learned that a Jew is somebody from the Southern Kingdom of Judah. This involves the tribes of Benjamin, Juda, and Levi. This is not the tribe of Judah—but the Southern Kingdom of Judah (3 tribes—Juda, Benjamin, and Levi). We could also include people from other nationalities who have converted to being a Jew. The book of Esther talks about people becoming Jews (converting to being a Jew). You can't change your nationality—but you can convert to being a Jew (as in belonging to the Southern Kingdom of Judah), or join the religion of Judaism. This is similar to how somebody today who belongs to one religion can convert to a totally different religion. Somebody who is not a Christian but converts to Christianity becomes a Christian. People could also move from one country (America) to another country (Canada). A person can become a Canadian or an American by joining the respective nation.

It has been my goal to provide the reader with a comprehensive understanding of who the 144,000 are. It should now be clear who this group is and what their purpose is. We must take these passages literally. God provides these details for a reason. We need to study these details extensively, and with an open mind. Saying "144,000 Jews" is actually not taking the text literally. The 144,000 comprises 12,000 male virgins each from the 12 tribes of the children of Israel. Many of these tribes don't exist today due to intermingling. It is impossible to claim the 144,000 are living Israelites who will get saved sometime in the last days. There is no feasible way for living Israelites to meet the specific criteria provided. Remember—the requirements for this group are: 12,000 male virgins (saved and righteous) from each of the tribes of the children of Israel. You'd be lucky to find these requirements in even one of the tribes listed (for example: 12,000 living virgin males from the tribe of Reuben).

What is the superior explanation?

The scriptures are clear. The 144,000 Israelites are **literally** 12,000 saved and righteous male virgins from each of the tribes of the children of Israel. The 12,000 saved male virgins of each of these tribes are **resurrected Old Testament saints**. These Israelites (who can easily meet the necessary criteria) will come back to the earth during God's Wrath period to act as a witness. This is because believers will have been raptured out of the earth. This is by far the best explanation. It doesn't require any farfetched storytelling and mental inventions. This interpretation (the correct interpretation) allows us to take the text and requirements literally. It also prevents any overgeneralizing of the text. We can be sophisticated and avoid sloppiness in our Bible exegesis.

We aren't forced to interpret the 144,000 Israelites as being modern day Israelites. The reason the details are provided is so we can understand these are literally 12,000 from each of the tribes mentioned, and these 144,000 (in total) will be resurrected as soul-winners when God pours out His wrath. The 144,000 came on the scene at the same time as the Rapture. They are sealed in Revelation 7, which is right before the rapture (the great multitude). How did they get to heaven before the rapture? They died in the Old Testament. This is a group that God picks in heaven that meet the criteria of being male virgins. After they are sealed, they will be placed on the earth. Today, we as believers do the soul-winning and evangelizing. But who is going to do this during God's wrath? The answer is simple: the 144,000 Israelites. We leave, they arrive, and let's not forget—they are immune to God's wrath. This makes perfect sense.

THERE ARE SOME STANDING HERE

The 144,000 saved Israelites are a worldwide ministry. They are present on this earth during God's wrath. They will be preaching the Gospel and helping to win the lost to the Lord. We also have the 2 witnesses who act as a local ministry. Their local ministry will be in Jerusalem:

Revelation 11:3-6

³ And I will give power unto **my two witnesses**, and they shall prophesy a thousand two hundred and threescore days, clothed in sackcloth.

⁴ These are the two olive trees, and the two candlesticks standing before the God of the earth.

⁵ And if any man will hurt them, fire proceedeth out of their mouth, and devoureth their enemies: and if any man will hurt them, he must in this manner be killed.

⁶ These have power to shut heaven, that it rain not in the days of their prophecy: and have power over waters to turn them to blood, and to smite the earth with all plagues, as often as they will.

I believe these two witnesses are Moses and Elijah. Notice in verse 6 these witnesses have the power to shut heaven—in order that it does not rain. Who had the power to do this in the Old Testament? Elijah. And who had the power over waters to turn them into blood? And to smite the earth with plagues? This of course is Moses (the plagues of Egypt). I believe these are some compelling correlations. Elijah caused it not to rain for 3.5 years. This is an attribute of Elijah. When we think of Moses, we think of the plagues of Egypt. The Exodus story of the Bible is one of the world's most famous stories. There have even been numerous movies made about this significant event in the earth's history. Moses performed many wonders—including the parting of the Red Sea.

The best line of evidence for why the two witnesses are most likely Moses and Elijah comes from Matthew 17:

Matthew 17:1-13

17 And after six days Jesus taketh Peter, James, and John his brother, and bringeth them up into an high mountain apart,

[2] **And was transfigured before them**: and his face did shine as the sun, and his raiment was white as the light.

[3] And, behold, **there appeared unto them Moses and Elias talking with him.**

[4] Then answered Peter, and said unto Jesus, Lord, it is good for us to be here: if thou wilt, let us make here three tabernacles; one for thee, and one for Moses, and one for Elias.

[5] While he yet spake, behold, a bright cloud overshadowed them: and behold a voice out of the cloud, which said, **This is my beloved Son, in whom I am well pleased; hear ye him.**

[6] And when the disciples heard it, they fell on their face, and were sore afraid.

171

⁷ And Jesus came and touched them, and said, Arise, and be not afraid.

⁸ And when they had lifted up their eyes, they saw no man, save Jesus only.

⁹ And as they came down from the mountain, Jesus charged them, saying, Tell the vision to no man, until the Son of man be risen again from the dead.

¹⁰ And his disciples asked him, saying, Why then say the scribes that Elias must first come?

¹¹ And Jesus answered and said unto them, Elias truly shall first come, and restore all things.

¹² But I say unto you, That Elias is come already, and they knew him not, but have done unto him whatsoever they listed. Likewise shall also the Son of man suffer of them.

¹³ Then the disciples understood that he spake unto them of John the Baptist.

Notice who appears at the transfiguration—Moses and Elias. Elias is Elijah. Elias is the New Testament way of saying Elijah. These are the two prophets that appear with Jesus on the mount of Transfiguration. This chapter is a continuation of the thought in the previous chapter—Matthew 16:

Matthew 16:28

[28] Verily I say unto you, **There be some standing here, which shall not taste of death, till they see the Son of man coming in his kingdom.**

This is a verse frequently abused by preterists. As a matter of fact, this verse is twisted by preterists to make one of their famous arguments. When the Bible says that some living in that generation will not pass away until they see the Son of man coming in His kingdom—it is referring to the transfiguration. This makes sense since there is no gap from Matthew 16:28 and Matthew chapter 17. We go right from Jesus saying this to the transfiguration on the high mountain in chapter 17. This is not coincidental. And yet preterists will abuse this text by saying Jesus must have come back in 70 AD since he said some will still be alive in that generation to see Him. The transfiguration in chapter 17 of Matthew is the fulfillment of Matthew 16:28. Jesus Christ is essentially giving them (Peter, James, and John) a glimpse of the coming of His glory. This is not the actual second coming of Christ. It is a preview. God does not want us to be confused—which is why we have the fulfillment of Jesus' words in Matthew 16 found in the very next chapter. If only preterists would continue reading. Preterists are guilty of isolating passages to support their indefensible position.

The preterist argument of Matthew 16:28 is further refuted by 2 Peter:

2 Peter 1:16-21

¹⁶ For we have not followed cunningly devised fables, **when we made known unto you the power and coming of our Lord Jesus Christ, but were eyewitnesses of his majesty.**

¹⁷ **For he received from God the Father honour and glory, when there came such a voice to him from the excellent glory, This is my beloved Son, in whom I am well pleased.**

¹⁸ **And this voice which came from heaven we heard, when we were with him in the holy mount.**

¹⁹ We have also a more sure word of prophecy; whereunto ye do well that ye take heed, as unto a light that shineth in a dark place, until the day dawn, and the day star arise in your hearts:

²⁰ Knowing this first, that no prophecy of the scripture is of any private interpretation.

²¹ For the prophecy came not in old time by the will of man: but holy men of God spake as they were moved by the Holy Ghost.

Peter is saying in verse 16 that he was an eyewitness of His (Jesus) majesty. Remember—it was Peter, James, and John that were on the mount with Jesus when He was transfigured. Verse 17 is an epic defeater of this common preterist talking point. Peter is referring right back to the transfiguration we just read about in Matthew 17. He is admitting that in this event—he heard a voice from heaven and this voice said, "This is my beloved Son, in whom I am well pleased." And yet you will still find preterists repeating this easily debunked talking point. Peter makes it clear—they were eyewitnesses to the power and coming of the Lord.

I don't believe it is a coincidence that it was Elijah and Moses standing with Jesus Christ on the mount where Peter, James, and John, got to see a glimpse into the coming of the Lord in His Kingdom. It makes sense that the two witnesses described in the book of Revelation are Moses and Elijah.

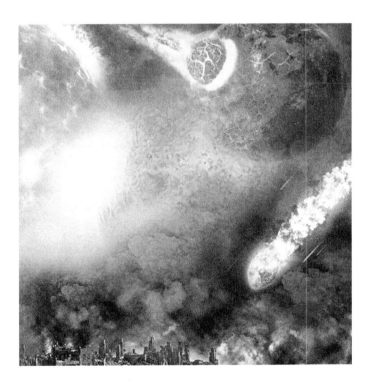

CHAPTER 4

AFTER THE TRIBULATION

God's wrath is not poured out until after the events of the 6th seal (sun and moon darkened). The breaking of the seals is giving us further details of the story that pertain to things that must come to pass. As each seal is broken, we get more and more of the story that ultimately leads up to the second coming of Jesus Christ. Essentially, as each one of the 7 seals are broken, a little bit more of the story becomes discernible to us. The story is not all given to us at once. It is given to us in increments which consistently match up to the events revealed in Matthew 24 (when the disciples ask Jesus when is He returning and what is the time of the end?).

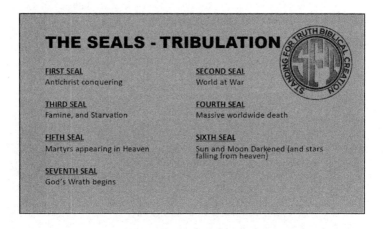

In Matthew 24, we get an entire chapter covering end times events. The information provided by Jesus Christ in this chapter is more important now than ever. This information is so incredibly important for believers to know and understand that it is also provided in Luke 21, and Mark 13. We need to understand these end times teachings. God's Word wants us to know these things even more as we see the day approaching. And today is closer than it was yesterday. We ought to be aware of these teachings. God does not want us to be unprepared. He wants us to be ready and have a clear understanding of the tribulation (covered in great detail in Matthew 24, Luke 21, Mark 13, Revelation 6, and Revelation 13).

Chapter 6 of Revelation (the opening of the first 6 seals) lines up perfectly with the events described in Matthew 24 (the Olivet Discourse).

The opening of the first seal reveals the Antichrist going out to conquer (which as we will see results in a ripple effect that is common during the build up to war and war itself):

Revelation 6:1-2

6 And I saw when **the Lamb opened one of the seals**, and I heard, as it were the noise of thunder, one of the four beasts saying, Come and see.

² And I saw, and behold a white horse: and he that sat on him had a bow; and a crown was given unto him: and he went forth conquering, and to conquer.

177

What we are seeing is what is referred to as the beginning of sorrows. We also see this in Matthew 24:

Matthew 24:5-6

⁵For many shall come in my name, saying, I am Christ; and shall deceive many.

⁶ And ye shall hear of **wars and rumours of wars**: see that ye be not troubled: for all these things must come to pass, but the end is not yet.

In verse 5 of Matthew 24, we know many will come who claim to be Christ. We also know there will eventually arise one major Antichrist—who will rule over the world—and who will act in the place of Christ. The elect will know he is a fraud. This is not a coincidence that when the first seal is opened in Revelation, the first event described is the Antichrist going out on a white horse to conquer. This matches up perfectly with the events described by Jesus in Matthew 24—which ultimately culminates in the rapture (gathering together of the elect when Jesus comes in the clouds). This also lines up amazingly with Revelation 6 where the sun and moon go dark—and the great multitude appear in heaven in Revelation 7. This is not coincidental or accidental. God wants us to know that the rapture is after the tribulation—and before God's wrath.

The first seal covers the white horse, the second seal covers the red horse, the third seal covers the black horse, and the fourth seal covers the pale horse. These horses are what many people know as being the four horsemen of the apocalypse. The 5th seal is where we see the souls under the altar—which are the souls of them that were martyred because of their faith in Jesus. When the sixth seal is opened—the sun and moon are darkened. And because this lines up so consistently with the events in Matthew 24—we know this is when Jesus Christ will come in the clouds to gather together His elect. We see evidence for this in Revelation 7 when a great multitude that no man could number appears instantly before the throne. They came out of great tribulation.

Chapter 6 of Revelation begins at the end times. This is the "hereafter" phase of John's vision. Chapters 4 and 5 of revelation are essentially a prelude of what's to come. Chapter 6 is the result of this lead up to the opening of a scroll that only Jesus can unseal. As Jesus Christ opens more and more of the seals, we are getting more and more of the tribulation period revealed to us. By the time we reach chapter 7, the seventh seal has not yet been opened (and therefore the wrath period has not yet begun). First, we get the 144,000 saved Israelites (Old Testament saints from all the tribes of Israel) sealed in their foreheads, then we get the rapture, and God's wrath begins (trumpets and vials.) This is why it is of utmost importance that we understand there is a key difference between the 7 seals, and the 7 trumpets and vials (which are both representative of God's wrath). The 7 trumpets and vials represent the pouring out of God's wrath—while the events of the seals are not God's wrath. It is also important to note that the trumpet and vial judgments occur simultaneously (not the vials after the trumpets but simultaneously). The first 4 trumpet judgments are revealed in chapter 8 of Revelation with the 5th and 6th trumpets being covered in chapter 9 (which are called woes). The pouring out of God's wrath (in terms of the first chronology which is Revelation 1 – 11) ends in Revelation 11. The seals (representative of the tribulation) are basically events depicting the wrath of the devil. This is the persecution of the devil. Why would God's wrath consist of the killing of martyrs? That makes no sense. This is because the seals are not representative of God's wrath—they are representative of the tribulation—with the great tribulation starting at the abomination of desolation.

The Bible describes many antichrists—but in the opening of the first seal, we get a picture of the one major Antichrist:

1 John 2:18

> [18] Little children, it is the last time: and as ye have heard that **antichrist shall come**, even now are **there many antichrists**; whereby we know that it is the last time.

Verses 5 and 6 describe the arrival of antichrists and eventual wars and rumors of wars. The first seal is the Antichrist going forth to conquer. And the second seal matches up perfectly with Matthew 24 with the wars and rumors of wars. The second seal talks about peace being taken from the earth—world war. The Antichrist is pretending to be Jesus, going out to conquer, which results in a great world war:

Revelation 6:3-4

[3] And when **he had opened the second seal**, I heard the second beast say, Come and see.

[4] And there went out another horse that was red: and power was given to him that sat thereon to take peace from the earth, and that they should kill one another: and there was given unto him a great sword.

We see this all lining up perfectly with Matthew 24. This world war could definitely be World War 3. It might be safe to say that when we see the world at war (for a third time), we may just be in the second seal. The conquering of the Antichrist could take place mostly behind the scenes. Therefore, it may not be possible to know when we are in the first seal—but I do believe it will be obvious when we are in the second seal.

Up to this point—we see the ordering of events revealed in both Matthew 24 and Revelation 6 as being:

Number 1 – Antichrist going out to conquer,

Number 2 – world at war.

The next event on the tribulation timeline is famine (there will be very little food to go around and whatever food is available will be very costly). The third seal has a black horse:

Revelation 6:5-8

[5] And when he had opened **the third seal**, I heard the third beast say, Come and see. And I beheld, and lo a black horse; and he that sat on him had a pair of balances in his hand.

[6] And I heard a voice in the midst of the four beasts say, A measure of wheat for a penny, and three measures of barley for a penny; and see thou hurt not the oil and the wine.

[7] And when he had opened **the fourth seal**, I heard the voice of the fourth beast say, Come and see.

[8] And I looked, and behold a pale horse: and his name that sat on him was Death, and Hell followed with him. And power was given unto them over the fourth part of the earth, to kill with sword, and with hunger, and with death, and with the beasts of the earth.

This is like working a 12-hour day and receiving a penny. This extreme shortage of food will mean that food is exceedingly expensive. A day's wage will only be enough to buy the absolute basics. The penny of the Bible is different from the penny we have today. We know from the Bible that a penny is a day's wage for an unskilled laborer out in the field. The Bible is saying that a measure of wheat is costing somewhere between 100 and 150 dollars. Could you imagine working all day (12 hours), and all you can buy is a measure of wheat? I want to once again mention this is the obvious ripple effect, or result, of world war (which happens after the Antichrist goes out to conquer which is essentially pre-war). The fourth seal is death on a massive scale.

The third seal we have is famine, expensive food, and inflation. Again—this all lines up perfectly with Matthew 24: Antichrist, war, famine, pestilences, and this is all the beginning of sorrows:

Matthew 24:7-8

[7] **For nation shall rise against nation**, and kingdom against kingdom: and there **shall be famines**, and **pestilences**, and **earthquakes**, in divers places.

[8] All these are the beginning of sorrows.

When we include the fourth seal we get: Antichrist, war, famine, pestilences, death, hunger, disease and mass death—all the ripple effects of war and tribulation.

In verse 9 of Revelation 6, the Bible tells us the fifth seal involves Christians being put to death for the cause of Christ (faith in Jesus Christ will result in persecution and tribulation). Believers will be delivered up to be killed—which is the same thing we see in Matthew 24—the antichrist going out to conquer, world war, famine, pestilences, and then martyrs—where Christians are being delivered up and killed. This is a time of tribulation—terrible things happening on the earth:

Revelation 6:9-11

⁹ And when he had opened **the fifth seal**, I saw under the altar the souls of them that were slain for the word of God, and for the testimony which they held:

¹⁰ And they cried with a loud voice, saying, **How long, O Lord, holy and true, dost thou not judge and avenge our blood on them that dwell on the earth?**

¹¹ And white robes were given unto every one of them; and it was said unto them, that they should rest yet for a little season, until their fellowservants also and their brethren, that should be killed as they were, should be fulfilled.

If you are taking the time to examine the progression of events in Matthew 24 and Revelation 6, you should see these are all the same events—culminating with the sun and moon being darkened—and the rapture (the gathering together of the elect in Matthew 24 and the great multitude in Revelation 7).

Remember—when the first seal is opened, the Antichrist goes out to conquer. When the second seal is open, the world is at war (a world war). The third seal we see famine, and the fourth seal there is pestilence and people are dying. It is then the fifth seal that we see Christians being martyred for their faith (indicating the devil's focus has changed and is now directed at believers). First, Satan persecutes mankind in general (conquering, world war, famine, etc.) and then shifts his focus to believers, which is the ultimate goal. The Antichrist has his power because of the devil (the dragon). The devil must first get power, and then he can persecute believers. This is connected to Revelation 6 where the souls under the altar are wondering when God is going to avenge them. This means God has not yet avenged those that have been killed during the tribulation. This tells us God's wrath has not yet begun (because the seals are not depicting God's wrath). God's wrath begins with the trumpet judgments—which occur after the great multitude appears in heaven (rapture). Notice the clear timeline and chronology?

When the sixth seal is open—the sun and moon are darkened, and the stars fall from heaven (falling like figs out of a fig tree). This is a major event that is prophesied all throughout the Bible:

Revelation 6:12-17

[12] And I beheld when he had opened **the sixth seal**, and, lo, there was a great earthquake; and **the sun became black as sackcloth of hair**, and **the moon became as blood**;

[13] And the stars of heaven fell unto the earth, even as a fig tree casteth her untimely figs, when she is shaken of a mighty wind.

[14] And the heaven departed as a scroll when it is rolled together; and every mountain and island were moved out of their places.

[15] And the kings of the earth, and the great men, and the rich men, and the chief captains, and the mighty men, and every bondman, and every free man, hid themselves in the dens and in the rocks of the mountains;

[16] And said to the mountains and rocks, Fall on us, and hide us from the face of him that sitteth on the throne, and from the wrath of the Lamb:

[17] **For the great day of his wrath is come**; and who shall be able to stand?

The reader may have noticed that the cause of the events revealed in the opening of the seals are not necessarily supernatural. They are basically the outcome of the Antichrist going out to conquer—which ultimately results in a world war—and the ripple effect of world war is famine, inflation, pestilences, etc. Most of what occurs in the seals is manmade—but what we see after the tribulation, in the trumpets and the vials, are supernatural events (plagues, God's wrath). Matthew 24 and Revelation 6 are both absolutely clear—the rapture comes after the tribulation and before God's wrath. Matthew 24 and Revelation sufficiently prove the pre-tribulation rapture is false, and the post-tribulation, pre-wrath rapture, is scriptural. Since the post-tribulation, pre-wrath rapture position is scriptural, it is also the truth. This is because God's word is true. Nothing written and revealed to

186

us in the Bible is accidental and without purpose. We must take the scriptures seriously—and since the Bible clearly teaches a post-tribulation, pre-wrath rapture, we must take this truth seriously. We must be ready, and we must be watchful.

Now that we've comprehensively covered the seals of Revelation 6 and also their perfect correlation to Matthew 24, I want the reader to once again visually examine the series of events (tribulation, rapture, wrath):

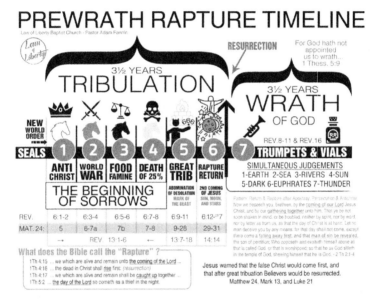

SOURCE: (2022). Lawoflibertybaptist.com. http://lawoflibertybaptist.com/prewrath.png

Note: Detailed chart found at the end of the book.

MATTHEW 24 REFUTES THE PRE-TRIBULATION RAPTURE

Proponents of the pre-tribulation rapture are forced to reject Matthew 24:29-31 as being the rapture (even though it obviously is). I covered this in chapter 1 of this book. I want to spend some time elaborating on why Matthew 24 is a major challenge to those that want to hold to a pre-tribulation rapture. The reason they are forced to twist these verses to say it's not describing the rapture is because verse 29 clearly states that the elect is gathering together after the tribulation—but they want to say the rapture takes place before the tribulation.

Pre-tribulation rapturists have struggled greatly with the entirety of Matthew 24. The elements found in verses 29-31 make it very evident that this is describing the rapture. Firstly—Jesus Christ is coming in the clouds—which is exactly what 1st Thessalonians chapter 4 (the famous rapture passage) describes as being a key element of the rapture (being caught up). The passage also talks about a trumpet sounding, and Jesus Christ gathering the elect (which many pre-tribulation rapture defenders argue is not talking about believers). Jesus Christ is gathering together His elect **"from the four winds, from one end of heaven to the other."**

Critics of the pre-wrath rapture who claim the "elect" in Matthew 24 is not referring to believers (they argue this to twist Matthew 24:29-31 to not be talking about the rapture) have invoked an incredibly weak argument. They will claim these verses are directed at Israel and the Jews—and not believers. In the New Testament—elect always refers to believers, or even Jesus Himself. We also see in verse 28 of Luke 21, it is believers who are being caught up and gathered together in the clouds with Jesus Christ:

Luke 21:28

²⁸ And when these things begin to come to pass, then look up, and lift up your heads; for **your redemption draweth nigh.**

Believers are waiting for glorified bodies (new bodies). This event in verses 29-31 of Matthew 24 (which we also see in Luke 21 and Mark 13) is describing the redemption of our (believers) bodies. This is clearly not talking about the Jews or Israel—and certainly not unbelievers. The elect being gathered together after the tribulation (when the sun and moon go dark) is undeniably describing believers. Again—it is believers (the elect—those with faith) that wait for new bodies (when somebody gets saved—their spirit is regenerated—not their body):

Romans 8:23

²³ And not only they, but ourselves also, which have the firstfruits of the Spirit, even we ourselves groan within ourselves, **waiting for the adoption, to wit, the redemption of our body.**

Matthew 24, Luke 21, and Mark 13 are clearly referring to the rapture (the culmination of the tribulation). We have Jesus coming in the clouds, a trumpet sounding, and the elect gathered. These are all the same elements we see in 1ˢᵗ Thessalonians 4:

1 Thessalonians 4:16-17

¹⁶ For the **Lord himself shall descend from heaven with a shout,** with the voice of the archangel, and with the trump of God: and the dead in Christ shall rise first:

¹⁷ Then we which are alive and remain shall be **caught up together with them in the clouds**, to **meet the Lord in the air**: and so shall we ever be with the Lord.

Another serious blow to the pre-tribulation rapture is the use of the second-person plural pronoun "you" when Jesus addresses His disciples in Matthew 24. When you are reading the Olivet Discourse, Jesus will say "you", "ye", "your". It is clearly the disciples and therefore Christians in view here (believers being persecuted during the tribulation). Notice it is the disciples that Jesus is saying shall be delivered up to be killed:

Matthew 24:9

⁹ Then shall they deliver you up to be afflicted, and shall kill you: and ye shall be hated of all nations for my name's sake.

When Jesus talks about Israel—He says "them". Why does Jesus' switch to a "them" when referring to the Jews in Matthew 24?

Matthew 24:15-16

[15] When ye therefore shall see the abomination of desolation, spoken of by Daniel the prophet, stand in the holy place, (whoso readeth, let him understand:)

[16] Then let <u>them</u> which be in Judaea flee into the mountains:

This is because the disciples Jesus is speaking with are the ones asking about the second coming of Christ:

Matthew 24:1-4

24 And Jesus went out, and departed from the temple: and his disciples came to him for to shew him the buildings of the temple.

[2] And Jesus said unto them, See ye not all these things? verily I say unto you, There shall not be left here one stone upon another, that shall not be thrown down.

[3] And as he sat upon the mount of Olives, **the disciples came unto him privately, saying, Tell us, when shall these things be? and what shall be the sign of thy coming, and of the end of the world?**

⁴ And Jesus answered and said unto them, Take heed that no man deceive <u>you.</u>

We see this very clearly in Luke 21:

Luke 21:20-24

²⁰ And when **<u>ye</u>** shall see Jerusalem compassed with armies, then know that the desolation thereof is nigh.

²¹ Then let **them** which are in Judaea flee to the mountains; and let **them** which are in the midst of it depart out; and let not **them** that are in the countries enter thereinto.

²² For these be the days of vengeance, that all things which are written may be fulfilled.

²³ But woe unto **them** that are with child, and to **them** that give suck, in those days! for there shall be great distress in the land, and **<u>wrath upon this people.</u>**

²⁴ And **<u>they</u>** shall fall by the edge of the sword, and shall be led away captive into all nations: and **<u>Jerusalem shall be trodden down of the Gentiles</u>**, until the times of the Gentiles be fulfilled.

We see the desolation of Jerusalem described in Zechariah 14:

Zechariah 14:1-2

14 Behold, the day of the Lord cometh, and thy spoil shall be divided in the midst of thee.

2·For I will gather all nations against Jerusalem to battle; and the city shall be taken, and the houses rifled, and the women ravished; and half of the city shall go forth into captivity, and the residue of the people shall not be cut off from the city.

Let me reiterate the importance of this point: the Olivet Discourse (Matthew 24, Mark 13, Luke 21) has Jesus using the second-person plural pronoun when referring to Christians. The Olivet Discourse also has Jesus using "them" to refer to Israel. Jesus has switched from "you" to "them". There is a clear distinction between Christians and Israel—and therefore the "elect" is clearly referring to Christians (believers). Again—if these passages were only talking to the Jews—why does Jesus' switch from a "you" (disciples/Christians) to "them"?

Jesus is answering the disciples' questions—and the disciples are believers in Him. Jesus also makes it clear in Mark 13 (parallel passage) that these sayings are not just for the Jews—they are for everybody:

Mark 13:37

[37] And what I say unto you I say unto **all**, Watch.

Mark 13:37 does not say "only to Israel". No—it says, "what I say unto you I say unto all, Watch." What part of "all" do the pre-tribulation rapturists not understand?

THE DAY OF THE LORD

The Day of the Lord is constantly associated with the sun and moon going dark. These are the signs that tell us the second coming is near. This is what we see in Matthew 24 when Jesus is describing His second coming.

The Day of the Lord is a day of punishment for the unsaved. It is the day of His great wrath. The Bible describes God's wrath being poured out on the same day Lot was taken out of Sodom and Gomorrah (when fire and brimstone rained down from heaven). God's wrath was also poured out on the same day Noah and his family went into the ark. Notice both Lot and Noah did not escape tribulation persecution. But they did escape God's wrath. This is the perfect picture of end times events. Believers will be on this earth for the tribulation period, but believers will be gone for God's wrath. The same day believers are removed from this earth, God's wrath will be poured down on the unbelieving world. The day Jesus Christ comes in the clouds to gather together His elect is the same day God will rain down fire and brimstone. The Day of the Lord will be a great day of destruction:

Isaiah 13:6-13

[6] Howl ye; **for the day of the Lord is at hand**; it **shall come as a destruction from the Almighty.**

[7] Therefore shall all hands be faint, and every man's heart shall melt:

[8] **And they shall be afraid: pangs and sorrows shall take hold of them; they shall be in pain as a woman that travaileth: they shall be amazed one at another; their faces shall be as flames.**

[9] Behold, **the day of the Lord cometh**, **cruel both with wrath and fierce anger**, to lay the land desolate: and he shall destroy the sinners thereof out of it.

[10] **For the stars of heaven and the constellations thereof shall not give their light: the sun shall be darkened in his going forth, and the moon shall not cause her light to shine.**

[11] **And I will punish the world for their evil, and the wicked for their iniquity; and I will cause the arrogancy of the proud to cease, and will lay low the haughtiness of the terrible.**

¹² I will make a man more precious than fine gold; even a man than the golden wedge of Ophir.

¹³ <u>Therefore I will shake the heavens, and the earth shall remove out of her place, in the wrath of the Lord of hosts, and in the day of his fierce anger.</u>

Joel 1:15

¹⁵ Alas for the day! for **the day of the Lord is at hand**, and as a **destruction from the Almighty shall it come.**

Now compare the above verses describing the day of the Lord with both **Revelation 6** and **Matthew 24** (the picture should be clear):

Revelation 6:12-17

¹² And I beheld when he had opened the sixth seal, and, lo, there was a great earthquake; and **the sun became black as sackcloth of hair**, and the **moon became as blood**;

¹³ And **the stars of heaven fell unto the earth**, even as a fig tree casteth her untimely figs, when she is shaken of a mighty wind.

¹⁴ And the heaven departed as a scroll when it is rolled together; and every mountain and island were moved out of their places.

<u>15.</u>And the kings of the earth, and the great men, and the rich men, and the chief captains, and the mighty men, and every bondman, and every free man, hid themselves in the dens and in the rocks of the mountains;

<u>16.</u>And said to the mountains and rocks, **Fall on us, and hide us from the face of him that sitteth on the throne, and from the wrath of the Lamb:**

<u>17.</u>**For the great day of his wrath is come;** and who shall be able to stand?

Matthew 24:29-31

²⁹ **Immediately after the tribulation** of those days shall the **sun be darkened**, and the **moon shall not give her light**, and the **stars shall fall from heaven**, and the powers of the heavens shall be shaken:

³⁰ And then shall appear the sign of the Son of man in heaven: and then shall all the tribes of the earth mourn, and they shall see the Son of man coming in the clouds of heaven with power and great glory.

³¹ And he shall send his angels with a great sound of a trumpet, and they shall gather together his **elect** from the four winds, from one end of heaven to the other.

THE ELECT

Since Matthew 24, Luke 21, and Mark 13 are so clearly teaching the rapture comes *after the tribulation*—those that say the rapture is before the tribulation (which is absolutely contrary to these passages) argue that the elect are not believers. They will claim the elect is actually Israel and the Jews. Some will argue Matthew 24 is a gathering together of the Jews into Israel during the last days. They will argue Matthew 24 isn't the rapture—it is actually Revelation 19 (the battle in Armageddon when Jesus Christ comes on a white horse—with His saints). These arguments are very weak—and I am about to demonstrate why.

Firstly—*the elect primarily refers to believers*—those who have trusted Jesus Christ for salvation:

Romans 8:33

³³ Who shall lay any thing to the charge of God's **elect**? It is God that justifieth.

Again—those who have believed and are therefore justified, and regenerated, are the elect.

Romans 3:24

²⁴ Being **justified freely by his grace** through the redemption that is **in Christ Jesus**:

Only the elect will not be deceived. Why would it make any sense to say unbelieving Israel will not be deceived by the Antichrist? Israel is already deceived—and will also be deceived by the Antichrist—but Matthew 24 makes it clear that believers (the elect) will not be deceived:

Matthew 24:21-24

[21] For then shall be great tribulation, such as was not since the beginning of the world to this time, no, nor ever shall be.

[22] And except those days should be shortened, there should no flesh be saved: but for the **elect's** sake those days shall be shortened.

[23] Then if any man shall say unto you, Lo, here is Christ, or there; believe it not.

[24] For there shall arise *false Christs*, and *false prophets*, and shall shew great signs and wonders; insomuch that, **if it were possible**, they shall deceive the very **elect**.

Only regenerated (to be regenerate means to be born again) believers can resist being deceived by false Christs, and false prophets. The elect here is not "Israel" since we know Israel is deceived. This verse tells us that it will be *impossible* to deceive the elect (believers). *Why would the elect in verse 24 of Matthew be different than the elect in verse 31?*

Matthew 24:31

[31] And he shall send his angels with a great sound of a trumpet, and they shall **gather**

together his elect from the four winds, from
one end of heaven to the other.

Believers don't deny that Jesus is the Christ:

1 John 2:22

²² Who is a liar but he that denieth that Jesus is
the Christ? He is antichrist, that denieth the
Father and the Son.

The elect are not antichrists. The elect is not referring
to unbelieving Jews. This makes no sense—and is found
nowhere in scripture—especially in Matthew 24.

Again—the elect is clearly referring to Christians:

Luke 18:7

⁷ And shall not God avenge his own **elect**,
which cry day and night unto him, though he
bear long with them?

Clearly—unbelievers don't count as God's elect.

Romans 9:11

¹¹ (For the children being not yet born, neither
having done any good or evil, that the purpose
of God according to **election** might stand, not
of works, but of him that calleth;)

We (believers) are elected by faith—and not by works.
It is by *faith alone in Jesus Christ alone* that we are saved and

are therefore the elect. The elect in Matthew 24 is referring to believers—this is undeniable. But of course—the pre-tribulation rapturists must invoke rescue devices in order to hold onto their false ideas of end times. These types of arguments are the best we can get.

Only the believing remnant of unbelieving Israel are regarded as the elect. *We see a clear distinction between Israel and the election*:

Romans 11:7

> [7] What then? **Israel hath not obtained** that which he seeketh for; but the **election hath obtained it**, and the rest were blinded.

I have never seen critics of the post-tribulation, pre-wrath rapture adequately address these verses—especially Romans 11:7—which makes a clear distinction between Israel (hath not obtained) and the election (hath obtained).

Only believers are the elect—and this includes the believing remnant of Israel. The believing remnant of Israel are not elected because they are of Israel. No—they are elect because they believe on Jesus Christ. Regardless of who you are—if you have trusted Christ as Savior—you are considered the elect. Believing Gentiles (as seen in Romans 8), and believing Jews (Romans 11), are both elect not because of their genetics, or nationality. They are elect simply because of their belief. This is the common denominator—belief and trust. The elect consists of all believers (Jew and Gentile).

Romans 11:5

[5] Even so then at this present time also there is a remnant according to the **election** of grace.

Colossians 3:11-12

[11] Where there is neither Greek nor Jew, circumcision nor uncircumcision, Barbarian, Scythian, bond nor free: but Christ is all, and in all.

[12] Put on therefore, as the **elect of God**, holy and beloved, bowels of mercies, kindness, humbleness of mind, meekness, longsuffering;

NOTICE: There is no difference positionally between Jews and Gentiles if they believe on Jesus Christ. When a person believes and trusts Christ for salvation—they are justified, regenerated, predestined for glorification—and they are the elect. Colossian Gentiles are being told that to be the elect of God is to believe on Jesus.

2 Timothy 2:10

[10] Therefore I endure all things for the **elect's** sakes, that they may also obtain the salvation which is in Christ Jesus with eternal glory.

Titus 1:1

1 Paul, a servant of God, and an apostle of Jesus Christ, according to the faith of God's

elect, and the acknowledging of the truth which
is after godliness;

The elect are those with faith in Christ Jesus. It is by
faith that we are considered the election of God. The nation of
Israel does not have faith in Jesus. But those individuals
within the nation of Israel that have believed in Jesus Christ
are deemed the elect. There exist nations that have turned
from God—but within those nations there is always a remnant
with faith. *It is this remnant that are the elect.*

1 Peter 1-2

1 Peter, an apostle of Jesus Christ, to the
strangers scattered throughout Pontus, Galatia,
Cappadocia, Asia, and Bithynia,

[2] **Elect** according to the foreknowledge of God
the Father, through sanctification of the Spirit,
unto obedience and sprinkling of the blood of
Jesus Christ: Grace unto you, and peace, be
multiplied.

A person becomes elect through the blood of Christ.
When somebody believes on Jesus—they have become the
elect. God foreknew who would believe, and He predestined
those that would believe (the elect) to glorification.

In verse 6 of 1 Peter 2, Jesus Christ Himself is referred
to as the elect. We as believers are elect because we are in
Christ:

1 Peter 2:6

⁶ Wherefore also it is contained in the scripture, Behold, I lay in Sion a chief corner stone, **elect**, precious: and he that believeth on him shall not be confounded.

Those that are not in Christ positionally are not the elect. You have to be born again—passed from death unto life (passed from a state of un-regeneration to regeneration) to be the elect. Remember—to those that have trusted Jesus Christ—there is no condemnation. Believers have been passed from death unto life. *They are in the life now.*

MATTHEW 24:29-31 IS NOT REVELATION 19

Before I cover the major reasons why Jesus Christ coming in the clouds to gather His elect in Matthew 24 is not the same event as Jesus Christ coming on a white horse in Revelation 19—I want to briefly recap several important points. I strongly believe a major reason why pre-tribulation rapturists have such a bad and sloppy view of end times is because they don't recognize the clear chronological order of Revelation (chapters 1 to 11 being in perfect chronological order and then chapters 12 to 22 in chronological order). They basically believe the seals, trumpets, and vials, are all happening at the same time with no real order to them. In reality—the seals come first, and then the trumpets and vials occurring during God's wrath period (simultaneously). They will frequently refer to Daniel's 70th week—the end times 7-year period—as 7 years of tribulation. They essentially believe the entire 7-year period is tribulation. This is found nowhere in scripture. We see a time of tribulation—with the latter end of the tribulation period being great tribulation. This is roughly the first 3.5 years of this 7-year period. Everything after the tribulation when the sun and moon go dark is no longer tribulation. That is why Matthew 24 says after the tribulation of those days! Everything before the sun and moon go dark is tribulation and everything after is God's wrath—which is roughly 3.5 years. The 7 year period culminates with the 1000 year millennial reign of Jesus Christ—when all of Israel (the Israel of God—spiritual Israel) will be saved.

I have described in detail the two-part chronological order of the book of Revelation. Chapters 1 to 11 are in perfect chronological order. We start with John on the Isle of Patmos in Revelation 1, we get the tribulation in Revelation 6, the rapture in Revelation 7, and God's wrath starting in Revelation 8.

When we get to chapter 12—we jump all the way back in time to the birth of Jesus Christ in the 1st century AD. This jumping back in time is exactly why we know the chronology has been restarted. We have the 1st century AD in Revelation 1—and then 1st century AD in Revelation 12. We should then logically expect the series of events after Revelation 12 to be the same as in Revelation 1-11—tribulation, rapture, wrath. It's no coincidence that we get the exact same sequence of events. The tribulation is in Revelation 13, the rapture is in Revelation 14, and then God's wrath begins in Revelation 15. Pre-tribulation rapturists do not understand this. As a matter of fact—most of those who hold to false eschatological positions (post-millennialism, amillennialism, preterism, etc.) also do not understand this clear two-part chronology of Revelation. This is key to sophisticated eschatology.

We see the same series of events from Revelation 1 to 11 and then Revelation 12 to 22. Again—the order is always the same: tribulation, rapture, and wrath. I know I have spent a lot of time on this specific point—but it is simply because of its importance. When you understand this important reality—you will begin to understand what the book of Revelation is teaching. It is no longer confusing when you read Revelation with this understanding.

Since we have the rapture in Revelation 7 and 14 with the great multitude in heaven and Jesus coming on a white cloud to reap the harvest of the earth—we should expect the tribulation right before this major event (rapture). This is exactly what we find. We get the tribulation in both Revelation 6 and 13. In Revelation 6, we see the exact same order of events that we get in Matthew 24. Antichrist goes out to conquer. Then we see wars, famines, pestilence, and the killing of Christians (martyrs). *After these things* we see Jesus coming in the clouds to gather His elect. This is after the sun and moon are darkened in Matthew 24.

Now that I've provided a thorough recap of these critical points, I want to dismantle the pre-tribulation rapture rescue device that argues Matthew 24 (when Jesus Christ comes in the clouds) is actually the event seen in Revelation 19 (when Jesus Christ comes on a white horse—with His elect—the saints). The reader should be able to see clearly why those in the pre-tribulation rapture camp (those that don't want to admit they're wrong) cannot admit that Matthew 24 is indeed the rapture. Many will argue Matthew 24 is a totally separate event than the rapture in 1st Thessalonians 4. Firstly—this is a bad argument since it contradicts the clear chronology of events I just reiterated in the previous paragraphs of this section. The battle in Armageddon does not occur until after the seals, trumpets, and vials. This battle occurs right before the millennial reign of Christ. Therefore, to argue Matthew 24:29-31 is Jesus coming on a white horse—rather than Jesus coming in the clouds to rapture the saints—is to completely contradict the chronology of end times events. This would place the battle of Armageddon immediately after the sun and moon are darkened—and after the tribulation (1st 6 seals of Revelation 6). But we know the battle of Armageddon where Jesus comes on a white horse to battle the Antichrist and his armies occurs roughly 3.5 years after the sun and moon go dark—since we still have God's wrath period (trumpets and vials). We know there exists a chronology (where the trumpets and vials follow the seals and the sun and moon going dark) because of phrases such as "after these things". Revelation 7 (where the great multitude appears in heaven) is after Revelation 6 (when the sun and moon go dark). There still exist numerous events before Jesus Christ comes back with believers for the battle of Armageddon in Revelation 19.

For those familiar with the Lord of the Rings trilogy—this extremely sloppy line of reasoning would be like arguing The Return of the King (the 3rd part to the Lord of the Rings trilogy) actually comes before The Two Towers (the 2nd part to the Lord of the Rings trilogy). No—The Return of the

King (and the events associated with that book and movie) comes after both The Fellowship of the Ring (the 1st part to this Trilogy) and The Two Towers. This should be basic. Pre-tribulation rapturists appear to confuse the basics. Again, understanding the chronologies of Revelation will help significantly to avoid serious errors. These are the types of serious errors that amillennialists, postmillennialists, preterists, historicists, and pre-tribulation rapturists are so frequently guilty of.

To claim that Jesus Christ coming in the clouds, and the trumpet sounding, is the same event as in Revelation 19 is completely absurd. There are almost no similarities between these two events. Pre-tribulation rapturists employ what is called *circular reasoning*. This is actually a logical fallacy. They will argue something like this: "we know the rapture comes before the tribulation, and so we know Matthew 24 can't be the rapture—since Matthew 24 says after the tribulation". Do you see why this is fallacious? They are assuming their position is true going into reading these important texts. Many are unwilling to see the text any other way. This is bad hermeneutics (Bible interpretation) because they are forcing their preconceived ideas into the text—rather than accepting what the text is saying.

We know Jesus Christ comes back on a white horse in Revelation 19 at the end of the 7-year period known as Daniel's 70th week. This is one reason why Matthew 24:29-31 cannot be talking about Revelation 19. There is far too much to happen in terms of events (trumpets, seals, destruction of Babylon, etc.) for this to be the case. But since pre-tribulation rapturists reject the obvious two-part chronology to the book of Revelation—they feel free to move around events any way they see fit (which is very sloppy and inconsistent). What I mean by this is they will take Revelation 19 (which is after God's wrath in terms of the series of events in Revelation) and place it right after Revelation 13 (the tribulation where the Antichrist rules and persecutes Christians). This is very bad Biblical hermeneutics. This is also why many pre-trib preachers actually avoid preaching on Revelation. Their blind acceptance of the pre-tribulation rapture fraud has prevented them from understanding what the book of Revelation is clearly saying and teaching.

There is almost nothing found in Revelation 19 (Jesus Christ coming on a white horse with His saints) that matches Matthew 24 (Jesus Christ coming in the clouds to gather His elect from the earth). Let's compare:

Revelation 19:11-14

[11] And I saw heaven opened, and behold a **white horse**; and he that sat upon him was called Faithful and True, and in righteousness he doth judge and make war.

[12] His eyes were as a flame of fire, and on his head were many crowns; and he had a name written, that no man knew, but he himself.

[13] And he was clothed with a vesture dipped in blood: and his name is called The Word of God.

[14] And the armies which were in heaven **followed him upon white horses**, clothed in fine linen, white and clean.

Matthew 24:29-30

[29] Immediately **after the tribulation** of those days shall **the sun be darkened**, and **the moon shall not give her light**, and **the stars shall fall from heaven**, and **the powers of the heavens shall be shaken**:

[30] **And then shall appear the sign of the Son of man in heaven**: and then shall all the tribes of the earth mourn, and they shall see the Son of man coming in the clouds of heaven with power and great glory.

[31] And he shall send his angels with a **great sound of a trumpet**, and they shall **gather together his elect** from the four winds, from one end of heaven to the other.

Now compare these 2 passages (Revelation 19 and Matthew 24) to the famous rapture passed in 1 Thessalonians 4:

1 Thessalonians 4:16-18

[16] For the **Lord himself shall descend from heaven with a shout**, with the voice of the archangel, and with **the trump of God**: and the dead in Christ shall rise first:

[17] Then we which are alive and remain shall be **caught up together with them in the clouds, to meet the Lord in the air**: and so shall we ever be with the Lord.

[18] Wherefore comfort one another with these words.

After examining all 3 passages—it should be absolutely clear that Matthew 24 and 1 Thessalonians 4 are the same event—while Revelation 19 is a totally different event. There exists a major difference between **Jesus coming in the clouds** and **Jesus riding a white horse.** There is no mention of a horse in Matthew 24 nor is there a horse in 1 Thessalonians 4 (the famous rapture passage). You'd think this notable distinction would be obvious? Apparently not.

Let's compare Matthew 24 and 1 Thessalonians 4:

- Trumpet sounds in both,

- Jesus Christ comes in the clouds in both,

- Jesus Christ gathers the elect in both.

Now what about Revelation 19?

- No trumpet,

- No clouds,

- The existence of a horse,

- No gathering together of the elect.

Another important aspect of the rapture that is surprisingly missing in Revelation 19 is the mention of the coming of the Lord. There is no word present in Revelation 19 that expresses this passage as the second coming of the Lord Jesus. This is because the second coming is found in 1 Thessalonians 4—and Matthew 24. The rapture is defined as the coming of the Lord—not Revelation 19 (battle of Armageddon):

2 Thessalonians 2:1-4

2 Now we beseech you, brethren, by **the coming of our Lord Jesus Christ**, and by our gathering together unto him,

[2] That ye be not soon shaken in mind, or be troubled, neither by spirit, nor by word, nor by letter as from us, as that the day of Christ is at hand.

[3] Let no man deceive you by any means: for that day shall not come, except there come a falling away first, and that man of sin be revealed, the son of perdition;

[4] Who opposeth and exalteth himself above all that is called God, or that is worshipped; so that he as God sitteth in the temple of God, shewing himself that he is God.

The rapture is not the coming of the Lord 1.5. No—the rapture is the second coming (His first coming was his birth in Bethlehem). Revelation 19 is never described as the coming of the Lord—or the second coming of Jesus Christ.

A final distinction between Matthew 24 and Revelation 19 is the fact that Jesus is gathering together the elect (believers) from the earth in Matthew 24—and believers (saints) are coming with Jesus in Revelation 19. And so, Matthew 24—the elect are on the earth when Jesus comes. And in Revelation 19—the elect are already with Jesus when he arrives on the earth for the battle against the Antichrist and his armies.

IS THE "TRIBULATION" FOR ISRAEL?

Defenders of the pre-tribulation rapture have employed some very feeble arguments. It has already been established throughout this book so far that the "elect" in Matthew 24 are clearly referring to believers. Jesus Christ is talking to his followers when describing the events of the tribulation—that culminate at the rapture near the end of the chapter. Pre-tribulation rapturists have attempted to argue for a rapture prior to the tribulation (even though this so-called pre-trib rapture is found nowhere in scripture) by claiming Daniel's 70th week is for Israel—and not Christians. Many believe this 7-year period of "tribulation" (even though the Bible never calls it the 7-year tribulation) is for the Jews, and to essentially bring the Jews to salvation through the judgment of God. Apologists of pretribulationism confuse tribulation and wrath (as we have discussed). Remember—we as believers are not appointed unto wrath—but we shall endure persecution, and we will not escape tribulation. To say the seals of Revelation 6 represent God's wrath is to claim the martyrs in heaven at the 5th seal got there because of God's wrath. This is absurd. The martyrs got to heaven because they were killed for the cause of Jesus Christ. Dying for our faith is not the result of God's wrath.

Is the "tribulation" for Israel—and the Jews? The answer is no. Daniel 12 answers this for us:

Daniel 12:1-2

12 And at that time shall Michael stand up, the great prince which standeth for the children of thy people: and **there shall be a time of trouble, such as never was since there was a nation even to that same time: and at that time thy people shall be delivered**, **every one that shall be found written in the book.**

[2] And many of them that sleep in the dust of the earth shall awake, **some to everlasting life**, and some to shame and everlasting contempt.

Verses 1 and 2 of Daniel 12 are describing the great tribulation (the final portion of the first 3.5 years of Daniel's 70th week), and the resurrection that follows this time of trouble. We understand from the Gospel of Matthew that this time will be cut short—and it will be cut short for the sake of the elect:

Matthew 24:22

[22] **And except those days should be shortened, there should no flesh be saved:**

214

but for the elect's sake those days shall be shortened.

Notice those days (the days of the great tribulation) are shortened—and if they weren't shortened—no **flesh** would be saved. This isn't talking about the believer's position. This isn't referring to spiritual salvation. What this verse is referring to is earthly, or physical salvation. Christians who endure to the end of the great tribulation (roughly 3 months) will be saved physically, since Jesus Christ will cut these days short by coming in the clouds to save believers:

Matthew 24:13

*13 But he that shall **endure unto the end**, the **same shall be saved**.*

Many have erroneously interpreted verse 13 of Matthew 24 as referring to positional salvation. A regenerated believer has both their position and their experience. Our position is secure in Jesus Christ, and is based on the finished work of Christ on the cross. Our experience on the other hand will depend on the believers' walk. This is why Paul encourages believers to walk in the spirit and not the flesh (Galatians 5:15). If we live in the spirit, we are to also walk in the spirit (Galatians 5:25). A believer's Christian life will be up and down, and the hope is that it is more up than down. Our experiential sanctification will depend on how much we choose to either walk in the flesh or walk in the spirit. Salvation, and our position, is based on faith and faith alone (Romans 4:5, Ephesians 2:8-9). This is how we are saved positionally, by faith in the finished work of Jesus Christ. Our experience as a believer on the other hand is based on our works.

The apostle Paul talks about the battle between the old man and the new man, or the flesh and the spirit (Ephesians 4:22-24, Colossians 3:10). When we walk according to the new man, we as believers will experience a sanctification process that is more up than down. And of course we will one day reach final sanctification (glorification), where we will no longer have this unregenerate flesh.

The reason a believer still sins after the moment of salvation is because of the flesh. The reason why salvation is a process is because we are currently being sanctified. It is appropriate to say (regarding salvation) that believers **"are saved"**, **"are being saved"**, and **"will be saved"**. The reason for this is because those that are regenerated (which comes by faith in Christ) are justified (just-as-if-I've-never-sinned), they are being sanctified (being "set apart"), and they will be glorified (final sanctification). Justification (a legal and forensic declaration that one is deemed righteous by faith) and regeneration happen the moment you trust Jesus Christ for salvation. Justification is a legal declaration. A believer is legally declared righteous. But believers are not taken up to heaven the moment they get saved. Christians still have a life to live, and a sanctification process to focus on. One day, we will be glorified.

Unfortunately—many Bible interpreters have looked to passages dealing with the experiential sanctification of a believer and have applied them (erroneously) to the position of a believer (which can result in a works salvation). And again—one of these misused passages is Matthew 24:13. But when you have a correct view of eschatology (the post-tribulation, pre-wrath position), you understand that this verse is describing temporal salvation. This verse is not adding "endurance" to salvation. What it is describing is our physical endurance to the end of the great tribulation where if we have not been killed—we will be caught up in the air bodily at the rapture. Wouldn't this be amazing? Believers who survive to the end of the great tribulation will never have to experience physical death. They will be caught up in the clouds and be changed in a moment:

1 Corinthians 15:52

52 In a moment, in the twinkling of an eye, at **the last trump**: for the **trumpet shall sound**, and the dead shall be raised incorruptible, and we shall be changed.

Considering this information—and going back to Daniel 12:1-2, we can see that those being delivered are the elect—believers. And believers will be delivered at the rapture. These are those written in "the book of life":

Daniel 12:1

12 And at that time shall Michael stand up, the great prince which standeth for the children of thy people: and there shall be a time of trouble, such as never was since there was a nation even to that same time: and at that time thy people

shall be delivered, **every one that shall be
found written in the book.**

Those that are written in the book of life positionally
are believers. Yes—everybody starts off in the book of
life—but those "found written in the book" are believers. If
somebody dies in an unregenerate state (not born again), they
are removed from the book—and are therefore not "found
written in the book". The tribulation is not for Israel—it is for
believers—and the tribulation period should strengthen
believers. This period should cleanse us. We are called to trust
in the Lord, and to be bold even in times of trouble. Our faith
should increase when we see the events of Daniel's 70th week
begin. Both Daniel and Revelation describe the Antichrist's
war as being against the saints. And Daniel 12 tells us it is
those "found written in the book" (the book of life) that will
endure this great trouble, and will be delivered. The saints
refer to believers. Those of us believers that have read our
Bibles, and understand what the signs of His second coming
are, should feel great comfort in knowing that Jesus Christ our
Lord has prepared us for this time of tribulation. We should
also feel confident knowing that the Antichrist—and the
dragon—will not succeed. They will not accomplish their
goals. The age of the Antichrist and the war against the saints
is the main focus of the final chapter of this book.

2 Corinthians 7:4

*4 Great is my boldness of speech toward you, great is my
glorying of you: I am filled with comfort, I am exceeding
joyful in all our tribulation.*

2 Timothy 1:7

7 For God hath not given us the spirit of fear; but of power, and of love, and of a sound mind.

Proverbs 3:5-6

5 Trust in the Lord with all thine heart; and lean not unto thine own understanding.

6 In all thy ways acknowledge him, and he shall direct thy paths.

CHAPTER FIVE

AGE OF THE ANTICHRIST

In the introduction of this book, I provided one of numerous fatal blows to a pre-tribulation rapture. This dismantling came from the second epistle of Paul to the Thessalonians:

2 Thessalonians 2:1-4

2 Now we beseech you, brethren, **by the coming of our Lord Jesus Christ**, and by our **gathering together unto him**,

[2] That ye be not soon shaken in mind, or be troubled, neither by spirit, nor by word, nor by letter as from us, as that **the day of Christ** is at hand.

[3] Let no man deceive you by any means: **for that day shall not come**, except there come a falling away first, and that man of sin be revealed, the son of perdition;

[4] Who opposeth and exalteth himself above all that is called God, or that is worshipped; so that he as God sitteth in the temple of God, shewing himself that he is God.

Paul is telling us (believers) to not be deceived by those who want to say the coming of the Lord Jesus (the rapture) can come at any moment—without any major signs leading up to it. Paul talked about the coming of the Lord in the first epistle of Paul to the Thessalonians:

1 Thessalonians 4:13-18

[13] But I would not have you to be ignorant, brethren, concerning them which are asleep, that ye sorrow not, even as others which have no hope.

[14] For if we believe that Jesus died and rose again, even so them also which sleep in Jesus will God bring with him.

[15] For this we say unto you by the word of the Lord, that we which are alive and remain unto **the coming of the Lord** shall not prevent them which are asleep.

[16] **For the Lord himself shall descend from heaven with a shout**, with **the voice of the archangel**, and **with the trump of God**: and **the dead in Christ shall rise first**:

[17] **Then we which are alive and remain shall be caught up together with them in the clouds, to meet the Lord in the air: and so shall we ever be with the Lord.**

[18] Wherefore comfort one another with these words.

I have seen many pre-tribulation rapturists attempt to argue that 2 Thessalonians 2 is not referring to the rapture (they might say it is referring to when Jesus comes on a white horse in Revelation 19). They argue this because they know if these important verses really are talking about the rapture (which they are) then they can no longer hold to a pre-tribulation rapture—since 2 Thessalonians 2 refutes it. Unfortunately for defenders of a rapture before the tribulation—both 1 Thessalonians 4 and 2 Thessalonians 2 refer to this event as the coming of the Lord. This isn't coming 1.5 or coming 3.0. No—this is the second coming of Jesus Christ. Paul describes the rapture in 1 Thessalonians 4 as the coming of the Lord and then next in 2 Thessalonians 2, he refers again to the coming of the Lord. In 2 Thessalonians, Paul makes it clear that the coming of the Lord cannot come until a great falling away, and the man of sin is revealed. The pre-tribulation rapture camp has no convincing response to this. Why would Paul tell us about events that are going to happen in the future if we aren't going to be there for them? The pre-tribulation rapture makes no sense of these key verses. The reason Paul is warning us about these events is because Paul wants us to know the rapture cannot occur at any moment—there are things that need to first happen. Pre-tribulation rapturists are incapable of getting around this reality (that the rapture comes after the tribulation).

It is important to note that the day of Christ and the day of the Lord is the same day. The day of Christ is referring to the day that we as believers receive the redemption of our bodies (the completion of our sanctification process—glorification). For believers—this is a great day. But

222

for the unbelieving world—this is a day of wrath—a day of judgment. Again—the day of Christ and the day of the Lord are simply 2 different names for the same day. When the day of the Lord is discussed—it's usually mentioned in the context of the unsaved and the judgment they will receive in the form of God's wrath (which believers are not appointed unto). Basically—in the context of those that are regenerated and justified, we are referring to the day of Christ, and in the context of the unsaved, we are referring to the day of the Lord (2 names describing the same day but in different contexts). As believers, we look forward to meeting our Lord and Savior Jesus Christ in the air. But to unbelievers—this will be a day of the Lord's wrath. This means unbelievers will see this from a different perspective than justified believers.

The rapture is called the coming of the Lord Jesus (as I have just proven). And we also see the rapture being described as our gathering together unto Him (*2 Thessalonians 2:1*):

2 Now we beseech you, brethren, **by the coming of our Lord Jesus Christ**, and by our **gathering together unto him**,

And in **1 Thessalonians 4:17**

¹⁷ Then we which are alive and remain shall be caught up together with them in the clouds, to meet the Lord in the air: and so shall we ever be with the Lord.

To claim this is not the same event is to simply not believe what these texts are saying and teaching. 1 Thessalonians and 2 Thessalonians clearly demolish a pre-tribulation rapture. It is a very desperate move to argue that the coming of the Lord in 1 Thessalonians 4 and the coming of the Lord in 2 Thessalonians 2 are 2 different events—even though they both describe our (believers) gathering together unto Jesus Christ. We also see these same similarities in Matthew 24 (which says the coming of the Lord comes after the tribulation—not before):

Matthew 24:29-31

[29] **Immediately after the tribulation** of those days shall the **sun be darkened**, and the **moon shall not give her light**, and the **stars shall fall from heaven**, and the powers of the heavens shall be shaken:

[30] And **then shall appear the sign of the Son of man in heaven**: and then shall all the tribes of the earth mourn, and they shall see the Son of man coming in the clouds of heaven with power and great glory.

[31] And he shall send his angels with a great sound of a trumpet, and **they shall gather together his elect** from the four winds, from one end of heaven to the other.

THE GREAT FALLING AWAY

There are some proponents of a rapture before the tribulation (disclaimer: many pre-tribulation rapturists have been adamantly against the use of this argument) that have employed an incredibly weak and desperate argument to save the day for the pre-trib rapture. They have said that the "falling away" (which clearly refers to falling away from doctrine and therefore spiritually—not physically) actually refers to the rapture. Right off the bat this makes no sense at all. These specific pre-tribulation rapturists are attempting to say that Paul is teaching "the rapture can't happen until the rapture happens". This argument is nonsense. It is laughable.

Pre-tribulation advocates that argue the **"falling away"** refers to the rapture is one of the most unreasonable arguments I have ever heard to support their position on end times. And I have heard a lot of arguments in my days engaging pre-tribulation rapturists (in debate, text and discussions—many of which can be viewed online). I want to point out the obvious: things don't "fall up". Falling away is not equivalent to being caught up! It's almost as if these specific defenders of the pre-tribulation rapture (again—this is just a select few that have chosen to employ this line of argumentation) simply invoked this argument to give pre-wrath proponents a healthy laugh.

I want to also point the pre-tribulation rapturists to something called "gravity". Earth's gravity keeps us on the ground and is a force that makes things fall. You can't fall up. Again—this argument is nonsense. But the fact some pre-tribbers have invoked this argument tells me they know how detrimental 2 Thessalonians 2 is to their views on eschatology. This is a final effort at saving the pre-trib rapture. And this final effort is a failure. These critics of the pre-wrath rapture are basically saying (indirectly) we can't trust anything the Bible says. Because if falling away actually means to be caught up—how can we trust any passage in the Bible? The answer is clear. The falling away does not refer to being caught up (the rapture). The Bible is not as cryptic as the pre-tribulation rapturists want to make it sound. No—these passages are very clear. What these people are good at is turning the plain reading of these scriptures on its head. Instead of believing what the Bible is saying—they would rather twist the clear meaning of these God inspired texts.

To further prove the "falling away" does not refer to the rapture—let us examine other instances of this in scripture:

Luke 8:13

[13] They on the rock are they, which, when they hear, receive the word with joy; and these have no root, which for a while believe, and in time of temptation **fall away**.

Is this the rapture? The answer to this question should be easy. Of course, it isn't! This verse is referring to a **spiritual falling away.** When somebody falls away spiritually—they are falling **down**—not **up**! This should be straightforward.

Hebrews 6:4-6

[4] For it is impossible for those who were once enlightened, and have tasted of the heavenly gift, and were made partakers of the Holy Ghost,

⁵ And have tasted the good word of God, and
the powers of the world to come,

⁶ If they shall **fall away**, to renew them again
unto repentance; seeing they crucify to
themselves the Son of God afresh, and put him
to an open shame.

Again—this is an example of falling away spiritually or
falling away from receiving the Gospel. This is not the
rapture. Remember—things don't fall up!

Going back to the Greek on this text is no help to those
that adamantly hold to a pre-tribulation rapture. The Greek
word for "falling away" is "apostasia". This just means
apostasy—falling away from the faith. This has nothing to do
with the rapture. This argument is grasping at straws. It must
be exhausting twisting the scriptures like this!

Even if we translated the verse with "the departure" rather
than "the falling away", it still would not help the
pre-tribulation rapture position. A departure suggests a
departing from the faith—departing from good doctrine. This
is what apostasy means.

1 Timothy 4:1-5

4 Now the Spirit speaketh expressly, that in the
latter times some shall **depart from the faith**,
giving heed to seducing spirits, and doctrines
of devils;

² Speaking lies in hypocrisy; having their conscience seared with a hot iron;

³ Forbidding to marry, and commanding to abstain from meats, which God hath created to be received with thanksgiving of them which believe and know the truth.

⁴ For every creature of God is good, and nothing to be refused, if it be received with thanksgiving:

⁵ For it is sanctified by the word of God and prayer.

This is a departure from the faith (apostasy) and not the rapture. This is referring to a believer that is falling from good doctrine to bad doctrine. Scripture interprets scripture. The Bible defines falling away as a spiritual departure. We should allow the Bible to define itself. Sound Biblical hermeneutics does not invoke making things up.

Where else is the word "apostasia" used?

Acts 21:21

²¹ And they are informed of thee, that thou teachest all the Jews which are among the Gentiles **to forsake Moses**, saying that they ought not to circumcise their children, neither to walk after the customs.

Acts 21:21 decimates this argument that claims the "falling" away means the "catching up". "Forsake" here in Acts 21:21 is the English translation of the Greek word "apostasia". As expected, (when we allow the Bible to define itself) this has to do with a **spiritual falling away** (notice: a falling down—not up). It is a massive stretch to say, "falling away" means "catching up"! This argument employed by some pre-tribulation rapturists needs to be completely discarded. I am thankful that some defenders of the pre-trib rapture have spoken out against this argument.

THE REVEALING OF THE ANTICHRIST

There will be a moment when we as believers understand exactly who the Antichrist is. This will be the official revealing of the Antichrist. As he goes out to conquer and comes to full power—it may not be immediately obvious who he is since much of this shift in power and rise to leadership could be behind closed doors. But when the Antichrist enters the temple, stops the daily sacrifice, and claims to be God—he will fully be revealed. There will be no question at this point—this is the Antichrist. Up to this point—there will most likely be many reasonable lines of evidence to help the elect understand who the Antichrist may be (prior to his full reveal in the third temple). Even today there are people making guesses as to who the Antichrist is. People are always trying to put the pieces together to understand who this eventual one world leader is. That is not to say any of these theories are true. My point is—there are always people coming up with theories (some even being wild and far fetched theories) on what they believe is the manifestation of Biblical prophecy. Therefore, when we enter Daniel's 70th week and the Antichrist begins to conquer and rise to power—there will no doubt be many theories presented that may or may not be right on who this leader is.

The moment we will definitely know who the Antichrist is has been described in scripture—and it is associated with what is called the abomination of desolation:

Matthew 24:15-16

¹⁵ When ye therefore shall see the **abomination of desolation**, spoken of by **Daniel the prophet**, stand in the holy place, (whoso readeth, let him understand:)

¹⁶ Then let them which be in Judaea flee into the mountains:

Paul describes this moment where the Antichrist enters the temple and desolates it. For full context—I will cite the whole passage again:

2 Thessalonians 2:2-8

² That ye be not soon shaken in mind, or be troubled, neither by spirit, nor by word, nor by letter as from us, as that the day of Christ is at hand.

³ Let no man deceive you by any means: for that day shall not come, except there come a

falling away first, and **that man of sin be revealed, the son of perdition**;

⁴ Who opposeth and exalteth himself above all that is called God, or that is worshipped; so that he as God sitteth in the temple of God, shewing himself that he is God.

⁵ Remember ye not, that, when I was yet with you, I told you these things?

⁶ And now ye know what withholdeth that he might be revealed in his time.

⁷ For the mystery of iniquity doth already work: only he who now letteth will let, until he be taken out of the way.

⁸ And then shall that Wicked be revealed, whom the Lord shall consume with the spirit of his mouth, and shall destroy with the brightness of his coming:

The man of sin, the son of perdition, in this passage is clearly the Antichrist. This is who needs to be revealed before the second coming of Jesus Christ will happen. Paul is telling us the Antichrist will sit in the temple and claim to be God. This is the context of the passage. I want the reader to focus in on a controversial verse in this passage (verse7):

⁷ For the mystery of iniquity doth already work: only he who now letteth will let, until he be taken out of the way.

Unfortunately—almost all pre-tribulation rapturists, and even many of those in the post-tribulation, pre-wrath rapture camp have this verse totally wrong. There are a lot of erroneous interpretations of verse 7. When we understand a few important things, and interpret scripture with scripture, the accurate interpretation of this verse, and the entire passage, can be easily understood. A correct understanding of this verse also helps us better understand the full scope of the last days—and the *dawn of the Antichrist*. I have seen bad interpretations of this passage on all sides of the eschatology debate—but I am going to reveal some serious truth about what verse 7 is saying.

Firstly—an accurate understanding of this passage involves knowing the "he" in verse 7 is a pronoun—and a pronoun has what is called an antecedent (discussed in chapter 2 with the "he" of Daniel 9:27):

> *grammar* : a <u>substantive</u> word, phrase, or clause whose denotation is referred to by a pronoun that typically follows the substantive (such as *John* in "Mary saw John and called to him")

SOURCE: *Definition of ANTECEDENT.* (n.d.). Www.merriam-Webster.com. https://www.merriam-webster.com/dictionary/antecedent

Basically—the antecedent is the word that goes before the pronoun. This is important because it tells the reader what the pronoun is. Without the antecedent—much of our daily interactions with people would be confusing. And much of scripture (and reading books in general) would be confusing. We would never know who is being talked about without an antecedent to inform us. For example: if I were talking with somebody, and I said "I have a friend named Matt. He does a great deal of the editing for Standing For Truth Ministries." The person I am talking to will understand that Matt is the editor that I am talking about. But if I came up to somebody and only said "he is an editor for Standing For Truth Ministries", this would make no sense. The person would have no idea who the "he" is. Or if I were talking to you and I said "he is a baseball player". You would ask "who is a baseball player?" This is because without the antecedent—this statement would confuse whoever I am talking to. The antecedent also helps prevent the need to constantly repeat the person's name I am talking about. For example: with an antecedent I do not have to say "Matt plays baseball. Matt is good at baseball. Matt hit 30 home runs this year." All I have to do is say Matt once—and then you know who I am talking about. This avoids redundancy in talking and writing. I don't have to keep repeating the name since you already know who I am talking about.

The pronoun "he" in the passage (2 Thessalonians) is taking the place of a noun. Again—every pronoun has a word that comes before it (antecedent) to tell us what that pronoun is. What most pre-tribulation rapturists, and unfortunately even some post-tribulation, pre-wrath rapturists want to do is look at the "he" in the verse and just insert whoever they want there. It is sloppy Biblical hermeneutics to just make stuff up by inserting anybody you want into this verse just because it says "he". If I were to take the approach of most pre-tribulation rapturists (since many like to argue the "he" is the Holy Spirit), I could equally say the "he" is Mickey Mouse, Batman, or even Iron Man. To avoid just inserting whoever we want in the passage when identifying who the "he" is, all we must do is look for the antecedent—which shouldn't be too difficult.

Now that we understand the importance of the antecedent—let us examine this passage in a sophisticated manner. Verse 6 has a "he":

> **⁶ And now ye know what withholdeth that he might be revealed in his time**.

Verse 6 is very basic. Who is the "he"? Well, the answer to that important question will be found in the answer to "who is being revealed in his time?" Please look back at verses 3 and 4 for the answer:

> ³ Let no man deceive you by any means: for that day shall not come, except there come a falling away first, and **that _man of sin_ be revealed**, **the son of perdition**;

> **⁴ Who opposeth and exalteth himself above all that is called God, or that is worshipped; so that he as God sitteth in the temple of God, shewing himself that he is God.**

The person being revealed is clearly the man of sin—the eventual Antichrist. Paul tells us exactly how he is revealed: by entering the temple, sitting in it, and claiming to be God. This is the point in time that we will know who the

Antichrist is. No more theories, no more guesses. We will know. As a matter of fact—there are a series of events at this same time that flow together in this epic reveal. The man of sin will receive a deadly wound to his head and that deadly wound will be healed. This will basically be a counterfeit resurrection—which makes sense since the devil always tries to do that which only God can do. Because of this "miraculous" healing, the Antichrist will claim to be God—and he will be worshiped as God in the flesh (when to believers he obviously is not God in the flesh). Many will declare him to be the second coming of Christ—which is again a reason why this topic is so extremely important. The pre-tribulation rapturists are waiting for the second coming of Christ—but the post-tribulation, pre-wrath rapturists know it is the Antichrist that will show up on the scene first. Those with a proper understanding of end times theology will not be fooled by this imposter. The world will worship him. The Jews will see him as their Messiah. But we as believers will not be deceived by him.

The Bible provides some amazing details on how and when the Antichrist will be revealed—and these details include the abomination of desolation. When this event takes place, we know this is not only the Antichrist, but also the start of the great tribulation (not to be confused with the tribulation). Remember—the tribulation is roughly 3.5 years, and the great tribulation (an aspect of the tribulation) is only a few months maximum. This is the moment the Antichrist, and the dragon (who gives power unto the beast) wages all-out war against the saints. This is when the devil shifts his focus to the saints—and the persecution of them (saints are believers). This is the endgame. The Bible explains how and why the Antichrist is revealed—and so many people have missed these important details—which is another reason why the writing of this book has been important to me.

With these details in mind—who and what is stopping the Antichrist from being revealed? Who needs to be taken out of the way in order for the Antichrist to step into the temple and claim to be God? What is preventing the abomination of desolation? Remember—we also have a "he" in verse 7:

⁷For the mystery of iniquity doth already work: only he who now letteth will let, until he be taken out of the way.

And when this "he" is taken out of the way—that wicked (Antichrist) will be revealed:

⁸ And then shall that Wicked be revealed, whom the Lord shall consume with the spirit of his mouth, and shall destroy with the brightness of his coming:

Here are some points we know:

-        The "he" being revealed is the Antichrist (that Wicked),

-        Somebody needs to be taken out of the way in order for the Antichrist to be revealed,

-        The revealing of the Antichrist will be when he enters the temple and claims to be God.

With these points—the answer to our primary question that pertains to "he who now letteth will let, until he be taken out of the way" should be easy to understand. The answer is the *human man of sin*. The man of sin needs to be taken out of the way (through a deadly wound to the head), in order that the dragon (Satan) can take control, and the "man of sin" comes back from the dead as the Antichrist—where he can now do what the Antichrist is supposed to do. I will back this up thoroughly with scripture. But before I do—I want to first go over a couple of the erroneous interpretations of this passage and show the reader why these interpretations simply don't work.

Pre-tribulation rapturists believe they can insert anybody they want as the "he" while completely ignoring the importance of the antecedent. Would God confuse us like this? Of course not. The answer to who the "he" is exists right in the passage itself. The "he" is the man of sin—who will be taken out—in order that the Antichrist can be revealed. And by his revealing—he will be worshiped as God. This is pretty simple. But the pre-tribulation rapturists have ignored this understandable answer and have claimed that "he" is actually the Holy Spirit—who they call the "restrainer". They have advanced a weak argument that says "the Holy Spirit is the restrainer and since the Holy Spirit is going to be taken out of the way, and believers are indwelt with the Holy Spirit, then that means the church will be taken out of the way aka the rapture before the tribulation!" Do you see how they completely run with this bad line of reasoning? Remember—2 Thessalonians is so absolutely detrimental to the pre-tribulation rapture deception that they have to perform some amazing mental gymnastics in order to avoid the obvious conclusion (the rapture is after the tribulation). The "falling away" argument doesn't work (we dealt with that earlier in this chapter) and this Holy Spirit argument doesn't work either. These arguments employed by apologists of the pre-tribulation rapture are rescue devices—plain and simple. They make no sense.

The first major problem with saying the Holy Spirit is the "he" in this passage (the restrainer) is that the Holy Spirit isn't mentioned anywhere in the passage! This means there is no justification for arguing that "he" is referring to the Holy Spirit. This is essentially just making things up. I can easily just say that "he" is referring to Batman. These are the leaps in logic I am all too familiar with in my time engaging pre-tribulation rapturists. Whoever the "he" is must be mentioned in the passage—or else we can simply insert whoever we want into the passage (as pre-tribulation rapturists and unfortunately some pre-wrath rapturists have done). Who is mentioned in the passage? The man of sin. Now that makes sense. But the Holy Spirit? No—that doesn't make sense. But no pre-tribulation rapture argument makes sense.

The second problem with this argument is the fact that the Holy Spirit is God! The Holy Spirit is the third person of the Holy Trinity. God is not just taken out of the way! God is literally everywhere:

Psalm 139:8-10

[8] If I ascend up into heaven, thou art there: if I make my bed in hell, behold, thou art there.

[9] If I take the wings of the morning, and dwell in the uttermost parts of the sea;

[10] Even there shall thy hand lead me, and thy right hand shall hold me.

It's like these pre-tribulation rapturists simply do not examine the rescue devices they employ. It would be so much easier if they were to just repent and admit they were wrong. It is refreshing to have the correct understanding of end times. But the pre-tribulation rapture is not just incorrect—it is incredibly sloppy, incoherent, and unsophisticated.

The Holy Spirit is never mentioned in 1st Thessalonians 1 or 1st Thessalonians 2 up to this point. We have seen absolutely no mention of The Holy Spirit. Therefore, there is zero justification for assuming the "he" is The Holy Spirit when we have yet to see The Holy Spirit mentioned in this passage. This would be an extremely confusing way of telling us the "he" is The Holy Spirit. They claim the "he" is the Holy Spirit and yet have no antecedent to demonstrate this is the case. Many pre-tribulation rapturists have even gone as far as saying this verse (that they claim is referring to the Holy Spirit) is evidence for a pre-tribulation rapture! It's mind boggling, I know. They will say this because the Holy Spirit is what allows things to happen and that's what "letteth" means. The Holy Spirit (according to their argument) is hindering the

Antichrist from being revealed. Let means to hinder and is parallel with the withholding. Basically—whoever this is (man of sin) will no longer be holding back or hindering the Antichrist from being revealed—since he will be taken out of the way. This actually makes sense. But the Holy Spirit? That makes no sense. Pre-tribulation rapturists have employed a line of argumentation that requires numerous logical leaps.

Another major issue with the "he" being the Holy Spirit involves salvation. If the Holy Spirit is removed according to the pre-tribulation rapturists—how do people get saved in their warped version of the tribulation? The Holy Spirit is required for people to get saved. It is he who quickens our spirits. You can't be saved without the working of the Holy Spirit—and therefore it again makes no sense to say that the Holy Spirit will be removed from this earth. We know from scripture people will be getting saved during the tribulation (3.5 years) and God's wrath (3.5 years). That is the whole point of the 144,000 Israelites who will be on this earth reaching people with the Gospel of Jesus Christ. The Holy Spirit is not taken out of the way. This argument is both absurd and borderline blasphemous.

THE MAN OF SIN

The context of 2 Thessalonians 2 is the revealing of the Antichrist and how the coming of the Lord Jesus Christ will not happen until this revelation takes place. The man of sin has to be taken out of the way before he can be revealed as the Antichrist. This revelation is when the Antichrist will set himself up as leader of the whole world. This is when he will officially be the one world leader—and begin his massive persecution against God's people—the saints. The human being (prior to the controlling or possession of the dragon) will be taken out of the way through a deadly wound to his head:

Revelation 13:3

³ And I saw one of his heads as it were **wounded to death**; and his deadly wound was healed: and all the world wondered after the beast.

The Bible makes it clear that the Antichrist is wounded to death and that he ascends out of the bottomless pit.

Revelation 17:8

⁸ The beast that thou sawest was, and is not; and **shall ascend out of the bottomless pit**, and **go into perdition**: and they that dwell on the earth shall wonder, whose names were not written in the book of life from the foundation of the world, when they behold the beast that was, and is not, and yet is.

Since the man of sin is mentioned, and the "he" cannot be referring to the Holy Spirit, then the "he" **MUST** be referring to the Antichrist—which ends up lining up perfectly when we interpret scripture with scripture. This is called sound and consistent Biblical hermeneutics. God cannot be taken out of the way—but man can. Therefore, the Antichrist will be taken out of the way prior to ascending out of the bottomless pit. The human man of sin needs to be killed in order that the evil spirit of Antichrist can take over (controlled or possibly possessed by the devil).

Revelation 17:8

⁸ The beast that thou sawest **was, and is not**; and **shall ascend out of the bottomless pit**, and **go into perdition**: and they that dwell on the earth shall wonder, whose names were not written in the book of life from the foundation of the world, when they behold the beast that was, and is not, and yet is.

The "is not" here is referring to somebody that was dead. "The beast that thou sawest was **(he was alive)** and is not **(he's dead now)** and shall ascend out of the bottomless pit." The Antichrist after the deadly wound—and after the false resurrection—is not really him anymore. This political leader will receive a deadly wound to his head. His dead body will be taken over by a spirit from hell. This spirit ascends out of the bottomless pit (the spirit of Antichrist). The Bible seems to be implying this spirit of Antichrist will control this man's body. Essentially—this man will function by the workings of Satan. I am not saying that the devil can resurrect life. Only God can do this. The devil is jealous of what God can do. Satan wants to be God. It's why he rebelled in the first place. Satan cannot create life—only God can. Therefore, this is not a true resurrection. The passage appears to be telling us that an evil spirit will be taking control of the man of sin's body. The real man of sin—that is—the human man of sin—is dead (he's been taken out of the way). The new man of sin is controlled by this evil spirit and the dragon/serpent (the devil). We could look at this like a false flag. The evil powers of this world want to take him out of the way in order to utilize his body for their own endgame. This is probably why these evil powers (with Satan as the leading force behind the evil powers of this world) wait until this moment (right before the abomination of desolation) to kill him and take over his body. This could be the moment the man of sin has reached near-full power. He has conquered. He has helped to start another world war (probably World War 3). And now the stage is set for him to take full power and full control over the world. Therefore, this could be the perfect moment for the dragon to take over. Of course—the devil has been influencing everything up to this point—but this is now the point the dragon will fully take over. This is the dragon's endgame. Which is why we see the sudden shift in focus. The focus is now on the saints. The one world government is now established, and the mark of the beast is being implemented—and anybody who does not take this mark—and worship the beast—will be killed. This is the devil's way of killing all Christians—those that will not worship the beast. This is how Satan can reveal who all the Christians are—those that refuse to worship him and his image. The dragon is using the man of sin's body as a vessel for the Antichrist and this vessel is being used for his final war against God and His saints.

The Antichrist is called the son of perdition. Who else is called the son of perdition? Judas Iscariot. Two people are referred to as the son of perdition in the Bible. The Antichrist and Judas. When Judas betrayed Jesus—the Bible says that

Satan entered him. This is what prompted Judas to betray Jesus. This is essentially what pushed Judas (who already had bad intentions and was basically an infiltrator) over the edge. This could be described as a moment of demon possession:

John 13:21-27

²¹ When Jesus had thus said, he was troubled in spirit, and testified, and said, Verily, verily, I say unto you, **that one of you shall betray me**.

²² Then the disciples looked one on another, doubting of whom he spake.

²³ Now there was leaning on Jesus' bosom one of his disciples, whom Jesus loved.

²⁴ Simon Peter therefore beckoned to him, that he should ask who it should be of whom he spake.

²⁵ He then lying on Jesus' breast saith unto him, Lord, who is it?

²⁶ Jesus answered, He it is, to whom I shall give a sop, when I have dipped it. And when he had dipped the sop, he gave it to Judas Iscariot, the son of Simon.

²⁷ **And after the sop Satan entered into him. Then said Jesus unto him, That thou doest, do quickly.**

Judas eventually regretted what he had done. He tried to give the money back to the chief priests, but they did not care. Judas then hung himself:

Matthew 27:3-10

³ **Then Judas, which had betrayed him,** when he saw that he was condemned, **repented himself**, and brought again the thirty pieces of silver to the chief priests and elders,

⁴ Saying, **I have sinned in that I have betrayed the innocent blood.** And they said, What is that to us? see thou to that.

⁵ **And he cast down the pieces of silver in the temple, and departed, and went and hanged himself.**

⁶ And the chief priests took the silver pieces, and said, It is not lawful for to put them into the treasury, because it is the price of blood.

⁷ And they took counsel, and bought with them the potter's field, to bury strangers in.

⁸ Wherefore that field was called, The field of blood, unto this day.

⁹ Then was fulfilled that which was spoken by Jeremy the prophet, saying, And they took the thirty pieces of silver, the price of him that was

valued, whom they of the children of Israel did
value;

¹⁰ And gave them for the potter's field, as the
Lord appointed me.

Judas was already a deceitful person—which left him
vulnerable to being utilized by the devil. He was stealing
money from the Ministry of Jesus. The Bible makes it clear
that Judas was never a believer. From the beginning—he did
not believe. This is a man vulnerable enough for Satan to enter
and use to his advantage. Judas was human—and because of
his humanity—he regretted what he had done to Jesus. But we
see a strong example of what the devil can do to somebody
who exists in a state of wickedness. Satan controlled Judas to
betray Jesus Christ. The Bible is clear—Satan entered into
him. Judas had a role to play—and so does the Antichrist. The
Antichrist has a massive role to play in the end times—which
might explain why Satan will completely take over his body
(after the human man of sin is taken out of the way). With
Judas—it was a temporary job—and therefore a temporary
possession. The Antichrist on the other hand will be the one
world leader. The world will worship him. He will be in power
for 42 months. And he will make war with the saints. This is a
different job than the job Judas had in betraying Jesus. This is
a job that the devil may want full control over. The way Satan
can have full control is not by a temporary possession—but
through the complete takeover of his body. In order to do
this—the human man of sin must die—and then the dragon
can take over. At this point—Antichrist (through the workings
of the dragon) will claim to be God—and the whole world will
wonder after him. This is the devil's final plan—his endgame.

This is why the so-called miracle—the fraudulent resurrection—needs to take place. The dragon knows this is an event that will make the entire planet worship him—with many falsely believing the Antichrist is the second coming of Christ.

This was a technical and comprehensive portion of this book. Let me reiterate a couple of the points for ease of understanding:

-       The man of sin is being revealed.

-       The man of sin is revealed by sitting in the temple of God and exalting himself as God.

-       He receives a deadly wound, the deadly wound is healed, and he is declared to be God in the flesh.

-       Many will be deceived into thinking he is the second coming of Christ—when in fact he is the Antichrist.

-       This is how the Antichrist will be revealed. The Bible makes it clear for us how the Antichrist is revealed, and how we can identify him.

WAR WITH THE SAINTS

Revelation 13:7-8

[7] And it was given unto him to make war with the saints, and to overcome them: and power was given him over all kindreds, and tongues, and nations.

[8] And all that dwell upon the earth shall worship him, whose names are not written in the book of life of the Lamb slain from the foundation of the world.

Revelation 13 is the famed chapter that describes the Antichrist's war with the saints. We must bear in mind it is the dragon—the devil—that gives power to the Antichrist. This is largely Satan's final war against God and His saints. Revelation 12 makes this obvious:

Revelation 12:17

[17] And the dragon was wroth with the woman, and **went to make war with the remnant of her seed**, which **keep the commandments of God, and have the testimony of Jesus Christ.**

Revelation 13 begins by depicting the beast with seven heads, ten horns:

Revelation 13:1-4

13 And I stood upon the sand of the sea, and saw **a beast rise up out of the sea, having seven heads and ten horns**, and **upon his horns ten crowns, and upon his heads the name of blasphemy.**

[2] **And the beast which I saw was like unto a leopard**, and **his feet were as the feet of a bear**, and **his mouth as the mouth of a lion**: and **the dragon gave him his power, and his seat, and great authority.**

[3] And I saw **one of his heads as it were wounded to death**; and **his deadly wound was healed**: and **all the world wondered after the beast.**

[4] **And they worshipped the dragon which gave power unto the beast**: and **they worshipped the beast, saying, Who is like unto the beast? who is able to make war with him?**

Much of what the reader has learned throughout this book will help make the final portion of this chapter incredibly understandable. The reader should already recognize the amazing similarities between verses 1-4 of Revelation 13 and what we discussed in the chapter on Daniel. Considering what we know about the book of Daniel (specifically chapters 7 and 8), it becomes clear as to what this beast is.

The animals mentioned in verse 2 are the same animals cited in Daniel 7—the leopard (Grecia), the lion (Babylon), and the bear (Medo-Persia). Daniel 7 also described the great beast—that represents the fourth kingdom (Rome in 1ˢᵗ century AD and the end times one world system). This final beast in Revelation 13 that is said to come out of the sea is the ultimate culmination of all the beasts that came before it (Babylon, Medo-Persia, Grecia, and Rome). The fourth kingdom does not come in peaceably. Many unbelievers like the idea of a new world order where everybody comes together in the name of peace. But this is not reality:

Daniel 7:23

²³ Thus he said, **The fourth beast shall be the fourth kingdom upon earth**, **which shall be diverse from all kingdoms**, and **shall devour the whole earth, and shall tread it down, and break it in pieces.**

This one world authority is described as devouring the whole earth and breaking it into pieces. Freedom is often taken away in the name of peace. The Antichrist will come into power deceitfully. The world will believe he is bringing the world together for the better. But we know this is not the case. The primary goal is full power, full control, and a war with the saints.

The beast represents both a kingdom and a king. This means the beast in Revelation 13 is representing the Antichrist (one world ruler) and the system (one world government). Some people have erroneously believed the beasts represent either a king or a kingdom. The truth is they represent both. The Antichrist is the king of the beast system.

We can see why a comprehensive understanding of Daniel and the prophecies of Daniel is extremely important (I recommend frequent referencing to Chapter 2—Daniel's 70 Weeks.) Remember—Jesus Christ came the first time during the Roman empire. He conquered spiritually. This conquering was accomplished through His death, burial, and Resurrection (and all who trust Jesus Christ for salvation will be saved). We are told His second coming will take place during the exact fulfillment of this fourth kingdom described in Daniel 7. This fourth and final beast represents a worldwide kingdom. And the ruler of this worldwide kingdom is the Antichrist. The end times beast system is a repeat of the Roman empire. The Roman empire was basically a foreshadowing of this final worldwide system. This is why the Antichrist's kingdom is said to be as robust as iron, will crush all opposition, and will essentially devour or take over the entire planet. The kingdoms prior to the first coming of Jesus Christ (Babylon, Medo-Persia, and Grecia) were never the devil's final plan. Neither was Rome the devil's endgame. No—the dragon's final war takes place during the reign of the Antichrist. Revelation 13 is what describes the endgame. Every single foreshadowing event in the Bible (especially in Daniel 7, 8, 11, and 12) is brought to culmination in this final worldwide

251

empire. This is the endgame. But will the dragon succeed? Of course not.

The Antichrist is the head of the Revelation 13 beast system. He is the little horn. He receives a deadly wound, that deadly wound is healed, and he is worshiped by the world. The dragon gives him power, and the false prophet convinces the world to worship him and to make an image of him. His 42-month reign starts during the second half of Daniel's 70th week—when he steps into the temple and claims to be God. This is when the abomination of desolation takes place. When the Antichrist gains full control—and becomes head of the one world kingdom—this is the fulfilling of the dragon's plan. The Antichrist's war against believers is the war that the devil has been planning for. But unfortunately for the devil—this war against the saints will be cut short when Jesus Christ comes in the clouds to gather together His elect.

This is yet another reason why the pre-tribulation rapture is a fraud. This war is against the saints—not "tribulation saints" (what pre-tribulation rapturists call people who get saved after the rapture). There is no pre-tribulation rapture (as this book has demonstrated). Christians will suffer persecution—and the end times persecution is at the hand of the devil and the Antichrist he gives power and authority to. But we as believers must not fear! God has not given His people the spirit of fear:

2 Timothy 1:7

7 For God hath not given us the spirit of fear; but of power, and of love, and of a sound mind.

Believers should glory in tribulation. God warns us we will suffer persecution—but to fear not. Some of us may be put into prison—and many of us will be killed. But we are overcomers. And we are overcomers because of our faith in the Lord Jesus Christ—who came to this earth (God manifest in the flesh) to die for the sins of the world. The Antichrist may be capable of killing us physically—and may even overcome us in this life—but he can never overcome us spiritually. If we as the elect are beheaded for the cause of Christ—great reward will await us. Paul prayed for boldness—and we should too. When we trust and love God—He will get us through trouble. We can be joyful even in persecution:

2 Corinthians 7:4

4 Great is my boldness of speech toward you, great is my glorying of you: I am filled with comfort, I am exceeding joyful in all our tribulation.

We will be victorious in the end. As powerful as the end times worldwide kingdom will be—it cannot stand against the Lord. To a believer—being killed by the Antichrist and his one world army is simply just being moved from one place (earth) to another (heaven). And when those days (the days of the great tribulation) are cut short (for the elect's sake) we will be glorified (receiving new bodies). This will be the time of God's wrath and judgment on this earth. Christians will be in heaven while the Antichrist and the unbelieving world endure the wrath of the Lamb. Just when the dragon (Satan), the Antichrist, and the false prophet (a false preacher in whom people are deceived into following) think they have won, Jesus Christ will come in the clouds, and we will be caught up to meet Him. This one world kingdom is predestined for destruction. It will lose:

Daniel 7:26-28

26 But the judgment shall sit, and they shall take away his dominion, **to consume and to destroy it unto the end.**

27 And the kingdom and dominion, and the greatness of the kingdom under the whole heaven, shall be given to the people of the saints of the most High, whose kingdom is **an everlasting kingdom,** and all dominions shall serve and obey him.

28 Hitherto is the end of the matter. As for me Daniel, my cogitations much troubled me, and my countenance changed in me: but I kept the matter in my heart.

THE FALSE TRINITY AND THE MARK OF THE BEAST

The devil loves to copy God. He wanted to be like the Most High:

Isaiah 14:12-14

[12] How art thou fallen from heaven, O Lucifer, son of the morning! how art thou cut down to the ground, which didst weaken the nations!

[13] For thou hast said in thine heart, I will ascend into heaven, I will exalt my throne above the stars of God: I will sit also upon the mount of the congregation, in the sides of the north:

[14] I will ascend above the heights of the clouds; I will be like **the most High.**

Just like how the one true God is a Triune God (Father, Son, Holy Spirit), the dragon will do his best to copy that. What do we see in Revelation 13? We see two trinities. We see a trinity of power—and a false trinity. The trinity of power is represented by the one world government, one world religion, and one world currency. We also see a false trinity being represented by the dragon, the Antichrist, and false prophet. In the past—we have predominantly seen local one world powers (governments or authorities that ruled the known world). This is what that great image—and the beasts represent: Babylon, Medo-Persia, Grecia, and Rome. And this final beast is a literal one world power. This is not just a local power that rules the known world. No—this is a one world system that rules the entire planet. With this final beast—we no longer see multiple sovereign nations. We see a world power that every nation is subject to. And this world power—and the rulers of it—force the world to take a mark. If this mark is not taken, you will be unable to buy or sell. This is a procedure made mandatory by the false trinity:

Revelation 13:15-18

[15] And he had power to give life unto the image
of the beast, that the image of the beast should
both speak, and cause that as many as would
not worship the image of the beast should be
killed.

[16] **And he causeth all, both small and great,
rich and poor, free and bond, to receive a
mark in their right hand, or in their
foreheads:**

[17] **And that no man might buy or sell, save he
that had the mark, or the name of the beast,
or the number of his name.**

[18] Here is wisdom. Let him that hath
understanding count the number of the beast:
for it is the number of a man; and his number is
Six hundred threescore and six.

The above verses describe the well-known mark of the
beast. This mark is in the hand, which therefore sounds like it
could be an implant of some kind (implantable microchip?).
We see this prophecy being fulfilled around us. Thousands of
years ago—people would have wondered how this was
possible. They would not have known how a mark could be
made mandatory and without it, you could not buy or sell. A
fulfillment of this prophecy would not have been feasible until
recent times. Therefore, when atheists—or even
preterists—scoff at futurists by asking where is Jesus—where

is His second coming? They'll frequently point to past generations that said Jesus Christ would come back during their lifetime. But again—the prophecies of Revelation could not have been fulfilled in the past—because the technology was not available until modern day.

Technology has now reached a point where it would be quite easy to eliminate cash. If people are primarily using cash or coins, it would be difficult to eliminate cash. This is because there is something called the black market where people can simply exchange money for products without doing it the proper way. If the false trinity and their beast system want all purchasing to be done through an implantable chip—a mark of some kind—they will have to eliminate cash altogether. This mark could be like debit cards today. Nowadays—it is very common for people to buy things at the store and simply tap their debit card as payment. This requires minimal effort, and no cash. All transactions could be done this way with an implantable chip. Given how far technology has come—it is not difficult to imagine a cashless society where all transactions occur electronically. The reader may even be thinking to themselves "I rarely use cash anymore". This is most likely a thought in most people's minds. Debit and credit cards are very convenient. And because of this convenience—huge multitudes of people are moving strictly to everything electronic.

A device that the majority of people have is a smartphone. You can pretty much do everything on a smartphone these days (which makes sense of the prophecy in Daniel that says in the latter days knowledge shall increase). You can do all your banking and purchasing over the smartphone. Clearly—we can see how the implementation of a mandatory mark (for buying and selling) can occur. We are witnessing Bible prophecy all around us. This is why the preterist position is laughable. You'd have to be living under a rock to not see where this world is heading. The Bible predicts a one world government, a one world religion, and a one world currency (the false trinity of power), and we are just one or two steps away from this! Apparently, this must all be a coincidence! Of course, it's not. This is the fulfillment of Bible prophecy. And the reason we are seeing the fulfillment of Bible prophecy is because futurism is true—and the various flavors of preterism are false.

You may be wondering "what about all of the cash floating around?" It wouldn't take long to deem paper money as being meaningless. There exists no intrinsic value in the paper we call money. This is precisely why we see many people today storing up gold and silver—since gold and silver actually has a use. But paper is essentially worthless—and could be deemed useless at any time by a one world leader and a one world authority. What this end times system will do is make paper money worthless—and move completely to electronic—where to buy and sell—you will require a mark. Without it, you will basically starve and suffer. They could sell this several ways. They could eradicate cash by convincing the world it's better for society. As with many things—the elites can make the claim that a cashless society is for peace and safety. Maybe paper money contains germs and will prevent the spread of highly infectious viruses. Or maybe a cashless society will stop the illegal buying and selling of drugs. Whatever the reason is—the Bible predicts this is coming. And we are living in a time when all of this is possible.

Many who argue for a rapture before the tribulation have challenged post-tribulation, pre-wrath rapturists by asking this question: *"what if believers take the mark of the beast?"* As a matter of fact—this was one of JD Morin's main arguments in my formal debate with him on the rapture. They will point out how born-again Christians can't lose their salvation—since Jesus Christ promised everlasting life to all those that believe (everlasting life means life that never ends). But we also know that all those who take the mark of the beast will be cast into the lake of fire. And so, what if a believer takes the mark? Do they lose their salvation? Do they go from life (spiritually) back to death? Aren't believers predestined for glorification after they believe and trust in Christ for salvation? Those who have trusted Jesus Christ for salvation are justified, regenerated, and will be glorified. They are eternally secure. Therefore, the answer to this challenge is simple:

Believers won't take the mark of the beast. This question is a hypothetical—and a hypothetical question deserves a hypothetical answer. I could ask the question: *what if I get abducted by aliens?* Or: *what if Santa Claus doesn't bring my children presents this year?* Just because somebody can ask a question does not mean it's necessarily a realistic question to ask. What does the Bible say about believers worshiping the beast and taking his mark?

Matthew 24:21-24

²¹ For then shall be great tribulation, such as was not since the beginning of the world to this time, no, nor ever shall be.

²² And except those days should be shortened, there should no flesh be saved: but for the **elect's** sake those days shall be shortened.

²³ Then if any man shall say unto you, Lo, here is Christ, or there; believe it not.

²⁴ For there shall arise false Christs, and false prophets, and shall shew great signs and wonders; insomuch that, **if it were possible, they shall deceive the very elect.**

The Bible makes it clear—Christians will not be deceived by the Antichrist—and will therefore not take the mark of the beast.

To get the mark of the beast—you must be willing to worship the beast. The mark of the beast is always associated with the worshiping of the beast. The real question we should be asking is: **what is the motivation of the Antichrist?**

Remember—the Antichrist is making war against the saints. This is the endgame for the false trinity. They want to find the Christians and kill them. The dragon wants to be like God, and he hates God's people. This is a final war against God and His people—the saints. His goal isn't to get

Christians to take the mark. The ultimate goal is to find out who the Christians are—and have them killed.

Okay—so what if Christians lie and pretend they are not Christian? Maybe a believer is worried they cannot feed their family—and out of pressure, and fear, they decide to take the mark by pretending to be willing to worship the beast (but in their heart and mind they know they won't). Again—what is the real motivation of the end times false trinity? It is to find the Christians—those that have been justified—the saints and kill them. If a believer wants to take the mark but is covertly disinclined to worship the beast (because they are hiding the fact that they are a believer), what good would this do for the Antichrist and his endgame? It would do no good—since he wants to physically remove Christians from this earth. Therefore, what could the false trinity (the dragon, Antichrist, and false prophet) implement as a way to filter out those that will actually worship the beast, and those that are only pretending? This answer is straightforward. We know we have the types of technology accessible to figure out who is lying and who is not. Perhaps, the Antichrist could carry out lie detector tests—or even put out some form of brain scan technology.

I want the reader to remember—this is a hypothetical question/challenge, and therefore it deserves hypothetical answers. The answers I provided are perfectly reasonable. But what do we know for sure? Well—the Bible is clear: those that get the mark must worship the beast—and the elect will not be deceived by the Antichrist (worshiping of the beast).

CONCLUSION

The events described in this book may at first appear intimidating—but as believers, we know who wins in the end. There will be a revealing of the Antichrist. He will be given power by the dragon (Satan), and they will have their one world government. This age of the Antichrist will not go on forever. As a matter of fact—those days will be shortened. And the Antichrist will suffer through God's wrath. The evildoers of this world will get exactly what they deserve. God is just and justice will be served. The Bible informs Christians about the last days and what will happen. God encourages believers not to fear those things that will be endured:

Revelation 2:10

¹⁰ Fear none of those things which thou shalt suffer: behold, the devil shall cast some of you into prison, that ye may be tried; and ye shall have tribulation ten days: **be thou faithful unto death, and I will give thee a crown of life.**

Jesus Christ comes back as Deliverer (the rapture), Judge (God's wrath), and Ruler (Millennium). Jesus is the ultimate superhero—the real superhero. And He will defeat the enemy.

We have God on our side. The enemy doesn't stand a chance. They can kill our bodies—but they can never kill our souls. If we as the saints die during the tribulation—we go to heaven and get to come back with Jesus Christ for the battle in Armageddon when He destroys the Antichrist and his army. If we survive the tribulation—and are caught up in the clouds when those days are shortened—we will go to heaven—and come back for the battle in Armageddon. Either way—we win. And either way, we come back with Jesus Christ for war against the Antichrist. Remember—we have overcome the world. He is greater than the world:

1 John 4:4

⁴ Ye are of God, little children, and have overcome them: **because greater is he that is in you, than he that is in the world.**

There will be no victory for the false trinity (the dragon, Antichrist, and false prophet). The saints are on the winning side. We are called to be both patient and faithful. And by faith, we know that in the end—the score will be settled. All the evil that has taken place on this fallen earth will be made right. Through our endurance—we will be rewarded. Salvation comes by the finished work of Jesus Christ. But our work done on this earth will be rewarded in the next life. This is one of the many reasons why it is important that believers walk in the spirit, put on the new man, and get to work for the Lord. We are called to be useful for God to further His kingdom. A believer that works hard and brings forth much fruit will have greater reward at the judgment seat of Christ. All Christians will be present for this judgment (a judgment not for heaven or hell—but for gain or loss of rewards). As believers—we should all want to hear these next words:

Matthew 25:21

²¹ His lord said unto him, **Well done, thou good and faithful servant**: thou hast been faithful over a few things, I will make thee ruler over many things: enter thou into the joy of thy lord.

When God is finished pouring out His wrath (trumpets and vials), the Word of God (Jesus Christ) will come back with all His saints (on white horses) to win the war and begin His rule:

Revelation 19:11-21

¹¹ And I saw heaven opened, and behold **a white horse**; and **he that sat upon him was called Faithful and True**, and **in righteousness he doth judge and make war.**

¹² His eyes were as a flame of fire, and on his head were many crowns; and he had a name written, that no man knew, but he himself.

¹³ And he was clothed with a vesture dipped in blood: and **his name is called The Word of God.**

¹⁴ And the armies which were in heaven followed him upon white horses, clothed in fine linen, white and clean.

¹⁵ And out of his mouth goeth a sharp sword, that with it he should smite the nations: and **he shall rule them with a rod of iron**: and **he treadeth the winepress of the fierceness and wrath of Almighty God.**

¹⁶ And **he hath on his vesture and on his thigh a name written, King Of Kings, And Lord Of Lords.**

¹⁷ And I saw an angel standing in the sun; and he cried with a loud voice, saying to all the fowls that fly in the midst of heaven, Come and gather yourselves together unto the supper of the great God;

¹⁸ That ye may eat the flesh of kings, and the flesh of captains, and the flesh of mighty men, and the flesh of horses, and of them that sit on them, and the flesh of all men, both free and bond, both small and great.

¹⁹·And I saw the beast, and the kings of the earth, and their armies, gathered together to make war against him that sat on the horse, and against his army.

²⁰ And the beast was taken, and with him the false prophet that wrought miracles before

him, with which he deceived them that had received the mark of the beast, and them that worshipped his image. *These both were cast alive into a lake of fire burning with brimstone.*

²¹ And the remnant were slain with the sword of him that sat upon the horse, which sword proceeded out of his mouth: and all the fowls were filled with their flesh.

Because of God—we will be victorious. We will not be defeated. Therefore, we should not be discouraged—or scared. We should delight in knowing what will come. Sadly, numerous Christians don't know the book of Daniel. They don't know the book of Revelation. They don't understand Matthew 24, Luke 21, and Mark 13. They aren't being taught these things. And they are being left unprepared and unwatchful. Not only do many Christians not know what to expect in the last days—and during Daniel's 70th week—they have been deceived into believing they won't even be here during this time! They have been taught that Jesus Christ could come at any moment with no signs and no warning. They are expecting the second coming before the rise of the Antichrist, and they are simply not prepared for the false trinity and their one world government. They will not be ready for the mark of the beast. And this is why this book is extremely important—especially in 2022—where we can see Bible prophecy being fulfilled all around us. The pre-tribulation rapture provides false hope. It is unscriptural and needs to be discarded. We will be here for the dawn of the Antichrist. As a matter of fact—this generation could very well be the generation that experiences these things. The stage is set for the age of the Antichrist. The stage is set for a one world government. And the stage is set for a mandatory mark that without it you cannot buy or sell. We should not fear these things—but we should know about them!

The path has been set for a New World Order—and the saints need to be ready for it. The end is rapidly approaching. By understanding the book of Revelation and what events await us in the future, we will not be perplexed and caught off guard when they begin to come to pass. When the world is at war, and the Antichrist rises, we will be ready to remain faithful to the end. We should sleep soundly knowing that in the end—Jesus Christ will set up His Kingdom on this earth—and we will rule and reign with Him. It is my hope and prayer that those who read this book will be encouraged and ready to face the last days. Truly, it should be counted as an honor to witness the grand finale of Bible Prophecy being fulfilled before our eyes. To think that God has chosen us to live through such a time as this should stir up the believer to greater works and zeal for Him. Take heart brother and sister, *if He be for us, who can be against us?* He is with us until the very end and knowing this, I want to embolden my brothers and sisters to be mentally, physically, and spiritually prepared. Not just prepared, but thrilled to watch the Bible's prophecies from thousands of years ago take place for we know that when the great tribulation starts, and the war against the saints intensifies, *Jesus will come quickly.* He will return and every eye behold Him and with His return, we will be rewarded for all that we have persevered through:

Revelation 22:20

²⁰ He which testifieth these things saith, **<u>Surely I come quickly</u>**. Amen. ***Even so, come, Lord Jesus.***

<u>**COMING SOON**</u>

<u>**PART TWO**</u>

END TIMES

REVEALED

THE WRATH OF GOD

DONNY BUDINSKY

STANDING FOR TRUTH
MINISTRIES

APPENDIX

DEBUNKING
HYPER-DISPENSATIONALISM

The contents of this section will thoroughly refute the false doctrine of dispensational salvation (different modes of salvation throughout history). Before I exclusively address the heresy that says people in the Old Testament were saved by a faith and works system—I will need to cover some essentials. I want to set a foundation that will allow the reader to best grasp why the false doctrine of dispensational salvation is essentially the result of dispensationalism in general. Those that would consider themselves "dispensationalists" would define a dispensation as "a length of time where God deals with men differently."

WHAT IS A DISPENSATION?

The Bible defines the word "dispensation" for us. And the Biblical definition does not resemble what dispensationalists ultimately teach. Let us have a look at what the Bible says about what a dispensation is:

1 Corinthians 9:17

[17] For if I do this thing willingly, I have a reward: but if against my will, a **dispensation** of the gospel is committed unto me.

A dispensation—according to the Bible—is something that is given—or *dispensed*. Paul is not arguing for different gospels ("hyper" dispensationalists argue for at least 3 different gospels) in different dispensations. In 1 Corinthians 9—Paul has been showing how it is appropriate for those who minister in the Gospel to be compensated for the work that they do (for example: a Pastor of a church). Paul wanted to preach the Gospel. Paul wanted to help win souls to Jesus Christ. His reward was being able to preach the Gospel, and he did it willingly. If it were against his will—he says, "a dispensation of the gospel is committed unto me." This verse has nothing to do with "different periods of time or ages" and "different modes of salvation".

Ephesians 1:9-10

⁹ Having made known unto us the mystery of his will, according to his good pleasure which he hath purposed in himself:

¹⁰ That in the **dispensation** of the fulness of times he might gather together in one all things in Christ, both which are in heaven, and which are on earth; even in him:

Paul was not used by God to bring another Gospel. Paul revealed important information that was hidden in the past. This information existed—but it was not yet known. More information is given or dispensed to men of God over time. Paul revealed (by God) more things about the original Gospel. Additional information was provided to Paul and Paul made this information known.

Ephesians 3:2-7

[2] If ye have heard of the **dispensation of the grace of God** which is given me to you-ward:

[3] How that by revelation he made known unto me the mystery; (as I wrote afore in few words,

[4] Whereby, when ye read, ye may understand my knowledge in the mystery of Christ)

[5] Which in other ages was not made known unto the sons of men, as it is now revealed unto his holy apostles and prophets by the Spirit;

[6] **That the Gentiles should be fellowheirs, and of the same body, and partakers of his promise in Christ by the gospel:**

[7] Whereof I was made a **minister**, according to the gift of the grace of God given unto me by the effectual working of his power.

It was Paul's purpose to make evident this valuable information:

Colossians 1:26-27

[26] Even the mystery which hath been *hid* from ages and from generations, but **now is made manifest to his saints:**

[27] To whom God would make known what is the riches of the glory of this mystery among

the Gentiles; which is Christ in you, the hope
of glory:

Paul in no way revealed a new Gospel. Paul was
merely revealing more about what formerly existed. There has
only ever been one Gospel—and one way of salvation. Not
every single detail was known about this Gospel, but God has
dispensed more of His plan to mankind over time. More
information being dispensed to man does not generate another
Gospel, or another age. The information being distributed or
dispensed over time is essentially more information given than
what was previously had. For example: there has only ever
been one God. Over time—God has revealed more about
Himself to man. Today—we know that God is one and yet
made of 3 divine persons (Father, Son, Holy Spirit). And there
is still much more to understand about the God of the
universe. Additional information about God will be dispensed
over time (in the Millennium, and the new heavens and new
earth).

1 Corinthians 13:12

[12] For now we see through a glass, darkly; but then face to
face: now I know in part; but then shall I know even as also I
am known.

When we see Jesus Christ in the flesh—it will be the
same God that has always existed. This will not be a new God.
But we will know more about Him. By faith we are saved. We
believe in Jesus Christ today. And one day more will be
revealed to us about the Triune God of the Bible.

273

God has always had one plan. There has always been one way of salvation. But more of this plan has been revealed, or dispensed, to man over time. This is what the word dispensation means. God has provided us another dispensation or has provided us more information about His original plan and purpose. Therefore, if this is what somebody means by dispensationalism—then there won't be an issue. But then we also need to ask ourselves *"should we even call ourselves dispensationalists—if this is all a dispensation means?"* I truly believe that nobody would call themselves a dispensationalist if they simply read the Bible for themselves and understood a dispensation as what the Bible describes.

The majority of dispensationalists reject what is called "hyper-dispensationalism", but this appendix will demonstrate that what is known as "hyper-dispensationalism" is the natural result of dispensationalism. Those that reject different modes of salvation in different dispensations but still consider themselves a dispensationalist are ultimately watering down the teachings of this false doctrine. It's best to toss out the whole system and come to a Biblical understanding of how God dealt with the Old Testament saints. This will be elaborated on later in this appendix.

Those that hold to a pre-tribulation rapture end up believing in a lot of other false doctrines. Pre-tribulationism results in a ripple effect of unbiblical doctrine and incorrect ideas. Many pre-tribulation rapturists simply recite talking points they have heard from their beloved preachers. And these preachers themselves are replicating concepts they've personally learned from other preachers—or in Bible College. These concepts are unscriptural—but are echoed because believing in a rapture before the tribulation requires a system that cannot be backed up by God's Word.

THE TIMES OF THE GENTILES

You will often hear pretribbers talk about "the church age" and "the times of the Gentiles". They believe we are currently living in what is called "the times of the Gentiles". To them—the end of this period is at the rapture. Basically, they believe it was all about Israel prior to this period known as "the church age" and after the rapture—we will enter another period of time where Israel is once again in focus. According to pre-tribulation rapturism, this "times of the Gentiles" is a period where God has largely put Israel on the shelf—and is now focusing on the Gentiles. And once this period is complete (the church age), God will go back to dealing with Israel (which is why they say the tribulation is all about Israel).

I have thoroughly refuted the pre-tribulation rapture model in this book—but I want to focus on a few additional points that demonstrate how unscriptural the pre-trib model is. What I mean by this is their basic starting points are wrong—and everything that flows from these starting points (the church age, times of the Gentiles) is the result of serious error and misunderstanding. The main reason I am saving some of these points for an appendix is because many prominent post-tribulation, pre-wrath rapturists still hold to aspects of dispensationalism (more on this later).

Pre-tribulation rapturism can be easily dismantled even without addressing some of these additional points. A person can hold (inconsistently I believe) to "the church age" and "the times of the Gentiles", and still reject pre-tribulation rapturism. They can still hold (as many do) to the true Biblical model of eschatology—which is the post-tribulation, pre-wrath rapture. Therefore, if you are interested in why it is unnecessary to hold to many of these pre-tribulationism claims and concepts if you are a pre-wrath proponent—then this appendix is for you. But if you hold to the pre-wrath model, and do not yet want to abandon some of the pre-tribulation rapture concepts I have mentioned—then you might not be ready for what I have to say in this section of the book.

Praise the Lord for all the Christians who have grown up believing in a pre-tribulation rapture and have now rejected it in favor of what the Bible actually teaches on the last days. But I understand there are certain concepts (such as dispensationalism) that many former pre-tribulation proponents simply do not want to give up—even though the most coherent and accurate view of end times theology comes by the correct understanding of these concepts (and not the warped pre-tribulation understanding of them).

Firstly—the church is throughout all the ages:

Ephesians 3:21

²¹ Unto him be glory in **the church** by Christ Jesus **throughout *all* ages**, world without end. Amen.

The New Testament *local church* is essentially a continuation—or a reformation—of the Old Testament *congregation*. There has always existed a spiritual nation of saints—believers. It was not revealed until the New Testament that the Gentiles would be a part of this spiritual nation of believers. This is all dispensation means—that more information has been dispensed to humanity over time. Those of Old Testament physical Israel who accepted Jesus Christ as their Lord and Savior continued in their faith. They continued in something that already existed. They remained true to their religion—which was always God's plan. Gentiles who believed on Christ (by faith) were grafted in among them. There is no Jew or Gentile in Jesus Christ. We are all one in our faith. The children of promise (those that have faith in Jesus Christ—just like our father Abraham) make up the Israel of God. To be a child of God, you must be a believer in the risen Lord.

Before I get into more detail on what the church is in the Bible—let's see what the Bible has to say about "the times of the Gentiles":

Luke 21:24

²⁴ And <u>they</u> shall fall by the edge of the sword, and shall be led away captive into all nations: and **Jerusalem shall be trodden down of the Gentiles, until *the times of the Gentiles be fulfilled.***

It is crucial that we don't just regurgitate what we have heard from our favorite preachers. We want to test what they are saying to the actual scriptures. We want to make sure we are reading the Bible for ourselves and seeing what God's Word says on all matters. Who will fall by the edge of the sword in verse 24 of Luke 21? This is the Jews. Third person pronouns are being used throughout Luke 21 (they shall fall by the edge of the sword, wrath shall be upon "this people", etc.). In other parts of Luke 21, we see the use of second person plural pronouns (you, your, ye). Verse 23 makes it clear that the wrath of God is on the nation of Israel:

Luke 21:23

[23] But woe unto them that are with child, and to them that give suck, in those days! for there shall be great distress in the land, and **wrath upon *this* people.**

Jesus is not talking to believers in verse 23. Christians are not appointed unto wrath. But at this time, there will be wrath upon the Jewish people. They will fall by the edge of the sword (not you—referring to believers and followers of Jesus Christ). The Jews in Israel at this time in Daniel's 70th week will be led away captive into all nations. Jerusalem shall be trodden down of the Gentiles, and this will occur until the times of the Gentiles be fulfilled. This is when the Antichrist steps into the temple and claims to be God. This is the abomination of desolation. This is essentially the moment the Antichrist betrays the people of Israel. The people wanted a third temple—and the Antichrist gave them their third temple. He made a deal with them. And then he double crossed them. He went against his word.

According to the Bible—what is the "times of the Gentiles"? This is a time when Jerusalem is trodden under foot of the Gentiles (the Antichrist's armies). This will be a time of wrath upon those in Israel responsible for aiding the Antichrist in his rise to power and the rebuilding of the third temple. This is supported by Chapter 11 of Revelation:

Revelation 11:2

2 But the court which is without the temple leave out, and measure it not; **for it is given unto the Gentiles**: and **the holy city shall they tread under foot forty and two months.**

Luke 21 described the time when Jerusalem will be trodden down of the Gentiles until the times of the Gentiles be fulfilled. Trodden is the past tense of tread. We see identical wording between Revelation 11:2 and Luke 21:24. The 42 months—or 3.5 years—ends when the Millennium begins (end of Chapter 11 of Revelation). At the same time the Antichrist declares himself as God in Jerusalem, the Antichrist's armies are brought in to desolate this city. God's wrath is upon the people who rejected the Lord Jesus Christ. The Jews have continually rejected Jesus Christ as Lord and Savior for more than 2000 years. Chapter 14 of Zechariah makes it clear that it is God gathering all nations against Jerusalem to battle at this time:

Zechariah 14:1-2

14 Behold, the day of the Lord cometh, and thy spoil shall be divided in the midst of thee.

> ^{2.}**For I will gather all nations against Jerusalem to battle**; and **the city shall be taken, and the houses rifled, and the women ravished; and half of the city shall go forth into captivity, and the residue of the people shall not be cut off from the city.**

This period when Jerusalem will be devastated and taken over by the Antichrist's armies will last 42 months—or 3.5 years. This occurs midway into Daniel's 70th week. It is incorrect—and unscriptural—to say that "we are in the times of the Gentiles". We are not in the times of the Gentiles—the times of the Gentiles occur approximately 3.5 years into this 7-year period and will last 42 months.

THE CHURCH AGE

Are we currently living in what many people call "the church age"? The answer is no. And I am going to explain why. Remember—*the church exists throughout all the ages.* Many dispensationalists believe that every Christian today makes up the church—the universal church. In the Bible—*church means congregation.* A congregation consists of a group of believers. This is an assembly of believers. We see evidence of this in chapter 2 of Hebrews:

Hebrews 2:12

¹² Saying, I will declare thy name unto my brethren, in the midst of **the church** will I sing praise unto thee.

This is a quote from the book of Psalms:

Psalm 22:22

²² I will declare thy name unto my brethren: in the midst of **the congregation** will I praise thee.

When the author of Hebrews (most likely Paul) quotes an Old Testament passage that uses the word "congregation", in the New Testament he uses the word "church". The reason for this is simple: *a church is a congregation.* An assembly of believers is considered a church, or a congregation. Are we congregated, or assembled, with all believers in the world? Of course not. We will not be assembled together with all believers until we are in heaven. What we have on this earth are local churches. We see this in Revelation chapters 2 and 3 (Ephesus, Smyrna, etc.). Rather than a universal church—what we have are local churches. This is not one major universal church—these are churches, plural. All around the world, there exist assemblies of believers (not one universal assembly—but multiple assemblies).

Jesus Christ is the head of the church. He is the head of every local church (*if it is a Biblical church*). Chapters 2 and 3 of Revelation provide local churches with an encouragement to improve—and to continue serving the Lord faithfully and diligently. Today, we have some churches that are fired up for the Lord, and other churches that are lukewarm. As followers of Jesus Christ—we need to carefully read Revelation 2 and 3 to know what might need changing. Churches (that are made up of believers, or saints) will know what not to do to become lukewarm. We should always have a love for evangelizing and soul winning.

Revelation chapters 2 and 3 describe literal local churches at this time that encompassed various strengths and weaknesses. The condition of these local churches can be applied to local churches today. There is nothing new under the sun. The strengths and weaknesses of local assemblies in the past are the same kinds of strengths and weaknesses present in local churches today. The principles given to these local churches (in Revelation 2 and 3) by Jesus Christ can be applied to local churches today.

SALVATION IN THE OLD TESTAMENT

Salvation has always been by faith and faith alone. There are some pre-tribulation rapturists who hold to a Biblical model of interpretation known as dispensationalism—or "hyper" dispensationalism. As I explained earlier—dispensationalism basically teaches that there were distinct dispensations (periods of time) where God worked with humanity differently (Abraham, Moses, the NT). According to them—there are 7 total dispensations. Those that I would define as being the "hyper" form of dispensationalism believe salvation was obtained in a different way in the Old Testament. They argue that salvation today (the dispensation of "grace") is by faith alone—but salvation in the Old Testament is by faith plus works. This is false. It is easily refuted.

The New Testament clearly tells us that salvation was also by faith alone in the Old Testament. If my filthy rag can't save me today—then how could my filthy rag save me in the past? If we could somehow be good enough—or have enough works—to be saved—then the finished work of Jesus Christ would be unnecessary. *Only the precious blood of Jesus Christ can save us.* A filthy rag cannot do the job. The truth is nobody is good enough to go to heaven by their own efforts. We aren't good enough to be saved by our own works today, and therefore we weren't good enough to be saved by our works in the Old Testament either. This false doctrine makes no sense. Jesus Christ is the Lamb slain from the foundation of the world. This means everybody who has ever gone (and will ever go) to heaven was by the blood of the Lamb (Jesus Christ).

Revelation 13:8

[8] And all that dwell upon the earth shall worship him, whose names are not written in the book of life of the **Lamb slain from the foundation of the world.**

Saints in the Old Testament looked forward to the cross while believers today look back to the cross. Either way—it's always been by faith in the finished work of Jesus Christ. Salvation is all about His death, burial, and Resurrection. One verse that absolutely dismantles dispensational salvation is found in the book of Acts:

Acts 10:43

[43] To him give **all the prophets witness**, that through his name whosoever believeth in him shall receive remission of sins.

This verse alone is enough to refute the claim that in different periods of time there were different modes of salvation (faith plus works). Acts 10:43 clearly states that all the prophets taught salvation by faith alone—salvation by believing on the Lord Jesus Christ. Hyper-dispensationalists want to say Old Testament saints were saved by faith and works—but this verse contradicts that claim. God's Word trumps the words of man any day.

There exist many flavors of Dispensationalism. Most people who hold to this doctrine do not subscribe to multiple Gospels. But the architects (Clarence Larken, John Nelson Darby, C.I. Scofield) behind this approach to Bible interpretation and understanding certainly taught different modes of salvation. In chapter 4 of Paul's epistle to the Romans—he dismantles this false idea that says there have been multiple modes of salvation:

Romans 4:1-9

4 What shall we say then that **Abraham our father**, as pertaining to the flesh, hath found?

[2] For if Abraham were justified by works, he hath whereof to glory; **but not before God.**

³ For what saith the scripture? ***Abraham believed God, and it was counted unto him for righteousness.***

⁴ Now to him that worketh is the reward not reckoned of grace, but of debt.

⁵ **But to him that worketh not, but believeth on him that justifieth the ungodly, his faith is counted for righteousness.**

⁶·**Even as David also describeth the blessedness of the man, unto whom God imputeth righteousness without works,**

⁷ Saying, Blessed are they **whose iniquities are forgiven**, and **whose sins are covered.**

⁸ Blessed is the man to whom the Lord will not impute sin.

⁹ Cometh this blessedness then upon the circumcision only, or upon the uncircumcision also? for we say **that faith was reckoned to Abraham for righteousness.**

In verse 2, Paul is clearly saying that *IF* Abraham were justified by works—it would <u>not</u> be before God. God is greater and holier than any human being. Our works will not justify us before God. Our works justify us before man. We as believers can be justified in the eyes of man by our works—but those works that vindicate us before man do not justify us before God.

Believers should want a productive faith—a profitable faith. A faith that does not work is a faith that will not benefit anybody. We want to be useful to God. By excelling in our *spiritual education* (discipleship, daily repentance, ongoing obedience, etc.) we will have a faith that is active—and a faith that is profitable to our fellow man.

Remember—man sees our works—but God sees our faith. Man looks at our life and our works. And it is our faith that justifies us before God. No flesh will be justified before God by the works of the law. We are called to believe, and then called to work for the Lord. This is why we are constantly commanded and encouraged to walk in the spirit, put on the new man, and get to work. Walking in the spirit (rather than the flesh) will prevent believers from becoming backslidden and experiencing times where they are dead in their Christian walk. We should want to be a blessing to others—and we will be a blessing to others when we are doers of the Word (and not just hearers only). When our fellow man sees our good works, and sees that inward change (regeneration, the indwelling of the Holy Spirit) manifested outwardly, we glorify our Father who is in Heaven.

Verse 5 of Romans 4 is one of the best verses proving justification by faith alone. I want the reader to notice that God is using both Abraham and David (verse 6) as an illustration of being saved without works. If both Abraham and David (who many dispensationalists would say existed in different dispensations) were saved by works—these illustrations would make no sense. Abraham and David are both from the Old Testament, and they are both portrayed as being saved by faith and not of works. Dispensational salvation is countered by the scriptures. It is unbiblical garbage.

Jesus Christ took all our sins upon Himself. He did all the work. His righteousness is imputed unto us when we believe on Him for salvation. Our sins (past, present, and future) were imputed unto Christ (notice the future tense in verse 8 *"will not impute"*). He took our punishment onto Himself. He is our substitute on the cross (substitutionary atonement). *Jesus Christ paid it all.* And simply by believing and trusting in Him—and His finished work, we can be saved. This is what Romans 4 is teaching. This is how we are saved today—and this is how people were saved in the past. Abraham was saved this way, and so are we today. Remember—*Jesus Christ is the Lamb slain from the foundation of the world.*

What is the blessedness of verse 6 of Romans chapter 4? The blessedness is not having our sins imputed unto us. We are not saved by our own righteousness. No amount of works—in either the Old Testament—or the New Testament—can save us. It is by His righteousness that we are saved. The righteousness of Christ is imputed unto the believer. This is the <u>dual blessedness</u> of being saved. Both Abraham and David had the dual blessedness that comes with believing on Jesus Christ and being saved. Abraham had the blessedness of being saved without works.

There is no way to get a faith plus works for salvation in Romans chapter 4. As a matter of fact—chapter 4 of Romans is demolishing a faith plus works system of salvation.

It is not that Abraham was "pre-law" (as some have said) that makes him saved by faith alone, since David was not "pre-law", and he also had the dual blessedness of the believer. David was saved by faith apart from works. David existed long after Abraham and Moses. He existed before Jesus Christ. And he was saved by faith alone. Notice how Abraham, David, and us as believers today, are all separated by long periods of time, and yet we are all saved the exact same way! And that way is not by works. One chapter alone has destroyed dispensational salvation. Romans 4 could not be any clearer.

The Bible teaches that Abraham was justified and therefore saved even before he was circumcised:

Romans 4:10-12

[10] **How was it then reckoned? when he was in circumcision, or in uncircumcision?** Not in circumcision, but in ***uncircumcision.***

[11] And he received the sign of circumcision, a seal of the righteousness of the faith which he had yet being uncircumcised: **that he might be the father of all them that believe,** though they be not circumcised; that righteousness might be imputed unto them also:

[12] And the father of circumcision to them who are not of the circumcision only, but who also walk in the steps of that faith of our father

Abraham, which he had being yet
uncircumcised.

Abraham was circumcised around 100 years old. This
means he was saved before his circumcision. And he also did
not offer up his son Isaac on the altar until long after his
circumcision. This means Abraham's justification that took
place when he offered up Isaac was a justification before
man—since he was already justified before God long before
this well-known event. This is why the entire world knows
Abraham as a great man of faith. Countless people have heard
of this story. Abraham was saved positionally prior to being
circumcised—but he was justified before man experientially
when he offered up his son Isaac on the altar. This is the faith
of Abraham being demonstrated or manifested to every
generation that reads this story in Genesis.

In verse 1 of Romans chapter 4—Paul is writing to the
Romans—and he calls Abraham *our father.* Then in verse 11
Paul tells us that Abraham is the father of all of them that
believe. *We are all (as believers) children of Abraham through
faith in Christ Jesus.* It has always been by faith. Salvation has
always been the same. It has never been of works. All
throughout the Old Testament we see righteous men of God
being saved by their faith and trust in the Lord. Abraham
believed God and he was saved through the righteousness of
Christ. Noah found grace in the eyes of the Lord. David called
upon the name of the Lord to obtain salvation.

There is and has only ever been one Gospel. There was
not a different Gospel in the Old Testament and a new Gospel
in the New Testament. This is false. And the scriptures

contradict this twisted doctrine. Those of the hyper-dispensational persuasion will even claim there will be another Gospel in the tribulation period. This is why they argue against a post-tribulation, pre-wrath model of eschatology by appealing to the mark of the beast. They claim that only a pre-tribulation, dispensational salvation view of scripture can account for how a believer can lose his salvation by taking the mark of the beast—since according to them—salvation is by faith and works in the tribulation. I have demonstrated in the final chapter of this book why believers won't take the mark of the beast—even if they were tempted by it. Therefore, this appendix is meant to refute the part of their argument that insists there are different modes of salvation—including a different mode in the tribulation (which is ridiculous).

The Bible is clear: there is one Gospel and anybody who preaches another Gospel is to be accursed. Paul, Jesus, and Peter all preached the same Gospel—and it has been a Gospel by faith alone in Christ alone. There are no contradictions in what the inspired authors of God's Word taught. They are all in perfect accord with each other.

Paul is preaching the Gospel of Jesus Christ and Jesus said whoever believes in Him has everlasting life. Jesus said you must be born again—and to be born again you must believe in Him. There is no ambiguity between Paul and Jesus. Jesus was preaching salvation by faith and faith alone even before His death, burial, and Resurrection.

In chapter 3 of Galatians—Paul makes it clear that Abraham was justified the same way as the Galatians are justified:

Galatians 3:1-8

3 O foolish Galatians, who hath bewitched you, that ye should not obey the truth, before whose eyes Jesus Christ hath been evidently set forth, crucified among you?

² This only would I learn of you, Received ye the Spirit by the works of the law, or by the hearing of faith?

³ Are ye so foolish? having begun in the Spirit, are ye now made perfect by the flesh?

⁴ Have ye suffered so many things in vain? if it be yet in vain.

⁵ He therefore that ministereth to you the Spirit, and worketh miracles among you, doeth he it by the works of the law, or by the hearing of faith?

<u>**⁶Even as Abraham believed God, and it was accounted to him for righteousness.**</u>

<u>**⁷Know ye therefore that they which are of faith, the same are the children of Abraham.**</u>

<u>⁸And the scripture, foreseeing that God would justify the heathen through faith, preached before the gospel unto Abraham, saying, In thee shall all nations be blessed.</u>

Paul asks the Galatians if they were saved by works, or by the hearing of faith? He makes the important point that Abraham was saved by faith—he believed God. And Abraham's belief was accounted to him for righteousness. Paul cannot be any clearer: we are not saved by works, and neither was Abraham. Verse 8 tells us the Gospel was preached unto Abraham. We find all throughout the scriptures people in the Old Testament being saved by faith. Abraham is called "faithful Abraham". Yes—we know more about Jesus Christ today than people in the Old Testament. More information has been provided to us over time. Those in the Old Testament did not know the name of Jesus. This had not been revealed to them. But they did know there was a Son of God, a Messiah, and a sacrifice. Isaiah 53 would have told them that the coming Messiah would be beaten and killed for the world. They may not have known every detail, but they knew who to put their trust in. They always knew to look forward to the Lamb of God that would be the Savior of the world. Chapter 3 of Genesis talks about the coming Savior who would bruise the head of the serpent. Those that called upon the name of the Lord in faith were saved. They may not have known exactly how the Savior would save the world—but they knew He would come, and they knew by faith in Him they could be saved.

There is one Gospel, and it is the same Gospel throughout all ages. God has always had one plan—but many of the details pertaining to His plan have not been known. God has chosen to dispense or to give more revelation of His plan over time. This is according to His pleasure. We exist in a day where much of God's plan has been unveiled to us. Old Testament saints obviously did not know as much about God's saving plan as we do today. Man has only ever been responsible for what information has been distributed to them. Hyper-dispensationalists do not understand this. They request those that reject dispensational salvation to show them the words "death, burial, and resurrection" in the Old Testament—which demonstrates their severe lack of understanding in how God revealed His plan of salvation throughout time. For example: when God made it clear in Genesis that a coming Savior (the seed of a woman) would bruise the head of the serpent (Satan), we today understand exactly who that was (Jesus Christ—the Son of God). Those that believed in the seed of a woman who would bruise the head of the devil—they believed in Jesus Christ. They did not know the name of Jesus Christ—but we today know the name, and we are held accountable for believing in that name.

It has always been the same mode of salvation. This is certain. Paul rebukes the Galatians for thinking they are saved by works. He makes this point by looking to Abraham and how he was saved.

Jesus Christ (God manifest in the flesh) came into this world to save sinners. His death, burial, and Resurrection is exactly why salvation is possible. Jesus is our only way to heaven. The New Testament refers to the Old Testament and tells us how they were saved. They were saved by faith—which is the same way we are saved today. Don't make your conclusions on what was true in the Old Testament based on what you think OT saints had available to them in terms of information—and books of the Bible. We can never really know for sure what scriptures the Old Testament people of God had available to them. This is because the scriptures were not only in written form back in the Old Testament. Much of God's Word was verbal. Dispensationalists oftentimes make the mistake of assuming exactly what Abraham knew based on what scriptures he had available to him. But they don't know what scriptures he had available to him—because again—much of God's Word was received orally.

Hebrews 1:1

1 God, who at sundry times and **in divers manners spake** in time past unto the fathers by the prophets,

God spoke in divers' ways through the prophets. There were many sermons preached in the Old Testament that were simply not written down. For example: Jude talks about Enoch preaching before the flood. Was this written down? No. But it was preached. And people heard it and learned it. The Bible tells us that Noah was a preacher of righteousness. But do we have Noah's sermons with us today? What did Noah preach? We don't know. But we know he preached, and we know people learned from him. His sermons were not recorded—but much of what he taught and preached eventually made its way into the books of the Bible. This is why we see many of the prophets preaching a lot of the same important teachings. God's Word has always been spoken—and it has always been powerful. The New Testament informs us the Old Testament saints (such as faithful Abraham) knew salvation was by faith. Therefore, it is false to say that the OT saints did not know that salvation was by faith and faith alone.

The first generation of humans on this earth were calling upon the name of the Lord to be saved:

Genesis 4:26

26 And to Seth, to him also there was born a son; and he called his name Enos: then began men to call upon the name of the Lord.

This verse also does not stop Abel, and Adam, from calling upon the name of the Lord. Verse 26 of Genesis 4 does not say "up until this point—nobody had called upon the name of the Lord". It is essentially telling us that when Enos was born—there began a great calling upon the Lord—as in—many began to be saved. And this is very early after the fall. Does Genesis 4:26 mention anything about works? Work your way to heaven to be saved? No it does not. This is because salvation has never been by works. It has always been by faith. Anybody who calls upon the name of the Lord (positionally) will be saved. Once we are saved—we can also call upon the name of the Lord for temporal or physical deliverance. But the calling upon the name of the Lord that takes place before the believer's experience begins is the salvific calling.

Genesis 12:8

[8] And he removed from thence unto a mountain
on the east of Bethel, and pitched his tent,
having Bethel on the west, and Hai on the east:
and there he builded an altar unto the Lord, and
called upon the name of the Lord.

Genesis 15:6

[6] And **he believed in the Lord**; and **he counted
it to him for righteousness.**

There has never been a day when man was saved by
works and by keeping the law. Nobody would ever come to
this conclusion (dispensational salvation) from the Bible
alone. As soon as Adam and Eve sinned—and man fell in the
Garden of Eden—salvation was always by grace. There is no
"one dispensation of grace". The dispensation of grace has
always been and will always be. Man has always been saved
by grace through faith and will continue to be saved by grace
through faith. In the Old Testament—God was saving people
by grace through faith in the same way God is saving people
by grace through faith today! The purpose of the law has
always been the same. The law is to show man that he is
exceeding sinful and therefore cannot save himself. The law is
like a mirror that shows us our need for a savior—and that
savior is the Lord Jesus Christ.

ABOUT THE AUTHOR

Donny Budinsky is the man behind the Team SFT YouTube Channel and Creation Ministry. He has authored the books *"The Endogenous Retrovirus Handbook - Dismantling the Best Evidence for Common Descent"*, *"The Independent Origins Handbook"*, *"Universal or Separate Ancestry? The Biblical Model of Origins Made Easy"*, *"Why Human Evolution Is False: The Scientific Case For Independent Origins"*, *"The First Couple: Adam and Eve – Independent Origins (Refuting the Critics)"*, and *"SPECIAL CREATION"*. In addition to these books, he has co-authored several books with creation apologist Matt N.

Donny has been studying creation and evolution for many years and has gained a significant following on YouTube. He has joined forces with Matt N. to help win the war against the philosophy of evolutionism. They have also been working for numerous years on formulating an irrefutable model on Biblical ancestry. They both work full-time defending the truth of Biblical creation.

Donny is no stranger to debates and defending Biblical creation. He has had 95+ live debates, including debates with many well known proponents of evolution, PhD Biologists, and serious students of evolutionary theory. He's been interviewed many times over various YouTube channels and podcasts and has himself interviewed some of the world's most well known young earth creationists and intelligent design advocates.

https://standingfortruthministries.com/

https://creationistclothing.com/

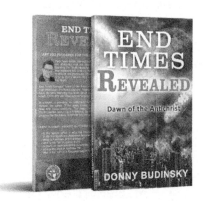

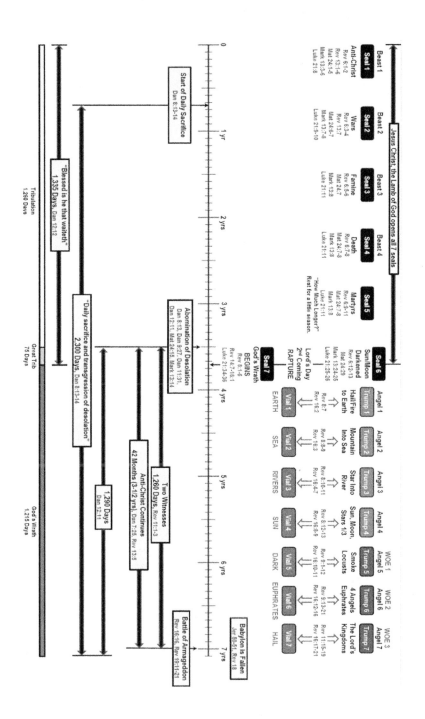

299

Matthew 24:29-31	Luke 21:25-28	Mark 13:24-27	Revelation 6:12-14	Revelation 7:9, Revelation 7:13-14
²⁹ Immediately after the tribulation of those days shall the sun be darkened, and the moon shall not give her light, and the stars shall fall from heaven, and the powers of the heavens shall be shaken: ³⁰ And then shall appear the sign of the Son of man in heaven: and then shall all the tribes of the earth mourn, and they shall see the Son of man coming in the clouds of heaven with power and great glory. ³¹ And he shall send his angels with a great sound of a trumpet, and they shall gather together his elect from the four winds, from one end of heaven to the other.	²⁵ And there shall be signs in the sun, and in the moon, and in the stars; and upon the earth distress of nations, with perplexity; the sea and the waves roaring; ²⁶ Men's hearts failing them for fear, and for looking after those things which are coming on the earth: for the powers of heaven shall be shaken. ²⁷ And then shall they see the Son of man coming in a cloud with power and great glory. ²⁸ And when these things begin to come to pass, then look up, and lift up your heads; for your redemption draweth nigh.	²⁴ But in those days, after that tribulation, the sun shall be darkened, and the moon shall not give her light, ²⁵ And the stars of heaven shall fall, and the powers that are in heaven shall be shaken. ²⁶ And then shall they see the Son of man coming in the clouds with great power and glory. ²⁷ And then shall he send his angels, and shall gather together his elect from the four winds, from the uttermost part of the earth to the uttermost part of heaven.	¹² And I beheld when he had opened the sixth seal, and, lo, there was a great earthquake; and the sun became black as sackcloth of hair, and the moon became as blood; ¹³ And the stars of heaven fell unto the earth, even as a fig tree casteth her untimely figs, when she is shaken of a mighty wind. ¹⁴ And the heaven departed as a scroll when it is rolled together; and every mountain and island were moved out of their places.	⁹ After this I beheld, and, lo, a great multitude, which no man could number, of all nations, and kindreds, and people, and tongues, stood before the throne, and before the Lamb, clothed with white robes, and palms in their hands; ¹³ And one of the elders answered, saying unto me, What are these which are arrayed in white robes? and whence came they? ¹⁴ And I said unto him, Sir, thou knowest. And he said to me, These are they which came out of great tribulation, and have washed their robes, and made them white in the blood of the Lamb.

300

Acts 1:9-11 "...a cloud received him out of their sight."	Revelation 1:7 "Behold, he cometh with clouds;"	Matthew 24:29-31 "...they shall see the Son of man coming in the clouds of heaven..."	1 Thessalonians 4:17 "...be caught up together with them in cloud, and in the clouds;"	Revelation 14:14-16 ", and behold a white cloud, and upon the cloud one sat like unto the Son of man,"
9 And when he had spoken these things, while they beheld, he was taken up; and a cloud received him out of their sight. 10 And while they looked stedfastly toward heaven as he went up, behold, two men stood by them in white apparel; 11 Which also said, Ye men of Galilee, why stand ye gazing up into heaven? this same Jesus, which is taken up from you into heaven, shall so come in like manner as ye have seen him go into heaven.	7 Behold, he cometh with clouds; and every eye shall see him, and they also which pierced him: and all kindreds of the earth shall wail because of him. Even so, Amen.	29 Immediately after the tribulation of those days shall the sun be darkened, and the moon shall not give her light, and the stars shall fall from heaven, and the powers of the heavens shall be shaken: 30 And then shall appear the sign of the Son of man in heaven: and then shall all the tribes of the earth mourn, and they shall see the Son of man coming in the clouds of heaven with power and great glory. 31 And he shall send his angels with a great sound of a trumpet, and they shall gather together his elect from the four winds, from one end of heaven to the other.	17 Then we which are alive and remain shall be caught up together with them in the clouds, to meet the Lord in the air: and so shall we ever be with the Lord.	14 And I looked, and behold a white cloud, and upon the cloud one sat like unto the Son of man, having on his head a golden crown, and in his hand a sharp sickle. 15 And another angel came out of the temple, crying with a loud voice to him that sat on the cloud, Thrust in thy sickle, and reap: for the time is come for thee to reap; for the harvest of the earth is ripe. 16 And he that sat on the cloud thrust in his sickle on the earth; and the earth was reaped.

Printed in Great Britain
by Amazon

44160538R00175